The Spirit of Thomism

The Spirit of Thomism

A *Wisdom and Discovery Book*

Under the theme "Wisdom and Discovery for a Dynamic World," Georgetown University marked the 175th anniversary of her founding (in 1789) with a varied program of lectures, conferences, and symposia on the key ideas and issues of our time. From the addresses and deliberations on these occasions, attended by noted scholars and experts on each subject, have come the volumes being published as Wisdom and Discovery Books.

The present volume consists of the 175th Anniversary Fenwick Lectures in Philosophy, delivered, under the auspices of the Department of Philosophy of Georgetown University, by Etienne Gilson, of the Pontifical Institute of Mediaeval Studies, the University of Toronto.

RILEY HUGHES
General Editor

The Spirit of Thomism

by Etienne Gilson

A Wisdom and Discovery Book

P. J. KENEDY & SONS · NEW YORK

Nihil obstat: Armand Maurer, C.S.B.
             Censor Deputatus

Imprimatur: Philippus F. Popock
             Archiep. Coadj. Torontinus

Toronto, July 20, 1964

Contents

The Spirit of Thomism

CHAPTER I

The Twofold Certitude

THE GENERAL TITLE of these lectures seems to announce a rather wide subject, but the spirit of Thomism is not Thomism. It is not the whole doctrine. If we follow the usual acceptation of the word, the "spirit" of a doctrine is the inspiring and animating principle that pervades and tempers it. That principle can be intellectual, emotional, or both, according to cases. In the present case, I think the true spirit of Thomism illumines a certain way to understand and practice theology, namely, the way of scholastic theology.

In order to avoid the peril of vagueness, I shall focus my attention on a small number of critical points commanding the interpretation of the whole doctrine. It is not my intention to justify Thomas on those points, and much less to preach them; my only desire is to clear up their meaning and

9

to make you understand them, at least to the extent that, after a life spent in familiarity with the doctrine, I myself have come to interpret their meaning. I sincerely hope that in my desire to serve it I shall not betray the authentic intentions of the Common Doctor of the Church.

How did Thomas Aquinas himself understand his doctrinal activities? What was he chiefly interested in as a teacher, as a writer, as a universally known and respected master in his own times? We all know he was a Christian, a priest, by vocation a friar and by function a professor of theology. But the same can be said of many others in the thirteenth century or, for that matter, in our own century. What is more proper to him is that as a professor of theology, Thomas Aquinas was—at the same time and *for the very same reason*—a passionate lover of philosophy.

Was his a unique case? I would not know, but I do know that it is not a universal one. Not all good Christians love philosophy. Leaving aside Saint Paul's indictment of the vain philosophy of the world (Col. 2:8), we still have to take into account the venerable tradition of all the ecclesiastical writers who expressed a resolute hostility against philosophy—for instance, Tatian, Tertullian, Arnobius, Peter Damiani and many others it would be easy to quote.

In our own time, all those who have personally

known Abbé Lucien Laberthonnière still remember that beyond Aristotle, it was philosophy itself he always hated in the doctrine and in the very person of Thomas Aquinas. Through many and cruel trials, Laberthonnière remained indefectibly faithful to the Church; yet he also lived in the unshakable conviction that one has to choose between being either a philosopher or a Christian. A faithful interpreter of his thought once summed it up in these terse words: "If Christianity contains the truth, then the rest does not contain it . . . our task is not to conciliate, but to choose."[1] I am not now challenging the value of that statement; my point is that no one who feels that way will ever find himself at home in Thomism, for indeed Thomas himself intended neither to choose nor to conciliate, but, rather to grasp the whole truth in the fullness of its all-embracing unity.

Far from seeing in Christian revelation the downfall of philosophy, Thomas Aquinas saw philosophy, in Eusebius of Cesarea's own words, as a kind of *praeparatio evangelica* by which divine providence prepared the minds of men to receive the truth of the Gospel. In a perhaps still more striking image—conceived as early as the end of the second century after Christ—Saint Justin held the astonishing view that God had given philosophy to the Greeks even as He had given his Law to the Jewish people.[2] Let us pause for a moment to assimilate the import of this statement. According to Justin, it was God's intention that philosophy should play for the Gentiles a role similar to that which his own revealed Law had played for the Jews. In other words, both the Greek philosophy and the Jewish Law were included in the general economy of the divine providence.

Now this exactly defines the constant attitude of Thomas Aquinas toward philosophy, particularly that of its best exponents, namely, Plato, Aristotle, and Plotinus among the ancients, and in modern times Avicenna and Averroes. While as late as the seventeenth century, Father Malebranche, a priest of the Oratory, was still to feel scandalized at the sight of Christian theologians allowing themselves to be seduced by the pagan philosophy of Aristotle, which he called "the philosophy of the snake," Thomas Aquinas often marveled, on the contrary, at its deeply religious inspiration. Judging from the metaphysics of Plato and Aristotle, Thomas Aquinas saw philosophy as bent upon the contemplation of God as the goal of human life: *omnes qui recte senserunt posuerunt finem humanae vitae Dei contemplationem.*[3]

Let us try to understand this correctly. Of course, Thomas does not mean to say that Aristotle anticipated the revelation of the Gospel. The

Philosopher could not guess that God himself would later on invite men to share, through grace, in his own beautitude. Aristotle had but a foggy notion of immortality and he knew nothing of the possibility of what we call future life. He never spoke of any happiness other than that accessible to man in this mortal life, yet he considered temporal happiness to be the supreme reward of a steady pursuit of philosophical speculation. That is the reason Aristotle assigned the intellectual contemplation of the highest intelligible objects as the supreme end of this mortal life. Now among such objects, God reigns supreme.

True enough, it is a far cry from the most perfect philosophical knowledge of the deity to the sight of God face to face promised to man by the Christian revelation. In fact, the distance is infinite, yet it is remarkable that Aristotle—going in the right direction as far as human reason unaided by revelation could possibly go—saw the whole of philosophical speculation as ordained to the kind of felicity man finds only in knowing God as he can be known through our scientific knowledge of nature: *et ad hanc (felicitatem) ordinatur tota cognitio philosophica.*[4] Nor was this a chance statement. At a later date, in more carefully weighed terms (because, after all, some parts of philosophy are less immediately related to God than others) Thomas will say that natural theology is the supreme part of philosophy, because philosophical inquiry is *almost* totally ordained to the knowledge of God: *cum fere totius philosophiae consideratio ad Dei cognitionem ordinetur.*[5]

Was this an illusion of perspective on the part of Thomas Aquinas? Or was Aristotle really convinced that the supreme end of man consists in the philosophical contemplation of the divinity? One thing at least is certain, and it is that to Aristotle the ultimate goal of human life was the conquest of happiness to be found in the steady practice of philosophical speculation. Such was to him the ideal life: not the search for truth, but its contemplation after it has been attained.

But even the mere searching for truth was to Aristotle a promise of happiness due to the favor of the gods: "He who exercises and cultivates his reason, seems to be most excellently disposed and, by the same token, to be a favorite with the gods. For if the gods care for man, as they are said to do, it is reasonable to think that they chiefly care for that in man which, being more akin to them, is also the best, namely the intellect. It is likewise reasonable to think that the men who thus cherish and cultivate that which, in themselves, is dearest to the gods, are living both right and nobly. Now, surely these qualities are those of the philosopher. So the philosopher is the man the gods prefer, and since the man the gods love best must also be the happiest, the philosopher must be the happiest of men." [6]

Far from finding fault with this notion of human blessedness, Thomas Aquinas never ceased to wonder at the truth of such a purely philosophical profession of faith. Here was a pagan philosopher who, following the light of natural reason alone, had discovered that there is something divine in intellectual knowledge and that its philosophical exercise is the surest way to blessedness. And why? Because the intellect itself is highest in human affairs (*optimum in rebus humanis*), nay, because the intellect is that in man which is most cognate to the gods, *cognatissimum*—a word which means, according to Thomas, that which in man is most similar to God: *id est simillimum Deo*. So Thomas concludes with Aristotle that to love the intellect is to love that which God prefers over all other things: *quid maxime amatur a Deo inter res humanas*.

At this point, I myself feel I have to stop. I cannot do more. It is up to you to do the rest. Or rather let us say: up to us, for in this I am one of you, a pupil listening to Thomas Aquinas and striving to understand what the master says. And my own question now is: If we were asked to name the supreme wonder of the world, how many of us would answer, "Intellectual knowledge"? Do we realize what a prodigy the existence of knowing beings actually is? Of all knowable things, knowledge itself is by far the most amazing there is.[7]

Sensation is the first wonder of the world. Think of the solemn moment in the history of the universe when under circumstances unknown to us the first eye opened to light. Then think of the far more solemn moment when for the first time an intelligent being conceived an abstract concept as standing for a plurality of individuals, and expressed it by a gesture or by some sort of grunt that was a word. At that very moment, all the future intellectual conquests of man in science and in philosophy were becoming possible. If there is nothing in nature more noble than the intellectual activity of man, it is small wonder that the steady pursuit of scientific and philosophical knowledge should lead the mind to the knowledge of God as its own origin and end.

Yes indeed—and the history of philosophy shows it—philosophical inquiry is almost totally ordained to the cognition of God as its end, but more remarkable still is the fact that Christ once said in the Gospel: "This is eternal life, that they may know thee, the only true God" (John 17:3). There is something amazing in this first coincidence of what philosophy says and what revelation teaches; but there will be other ones.

To recapture that feeling of unity between two distinct sources of knowledge is a first step toward a proper understanding of the spirit of Thomism. In order to confirm ourselves in that feeling, let us try to discover the origin of their unity.

Thomas not only loves and admires the intellect, he trusts it implicitly. There is in him no trace of the sophisticated relativism or quasi-skepticism of so many philosophers and scientists of today. Strangely enough, the reason for this difference was a religious one. Thomas Aquinas entertained the deep-seated conviction that to cultivate science and philosophy was to be about God's own business. He felt certain that all that is true for man owes its invincible certitude to the fact that it first is true for God. I know of no stronger expression of that conviction than the passage of the *Contra gentiles* (I, 7, 2) in which Thomas says that the knowledge of the first principles evident to the mind has been implanted in us by God, who is the author of our nature. This is the reason they cannot possibly not be true, since the very same principles from which human knowledge is derived, are likewise contained in the wisdom of God. An astounding statement indeed! *Haec ergo principia etiam divina sapientia continet.*

Some of our contemporaries love to speak of the utter relativity of human knowledge. They think that what is true to us could appear untrue in the light of a differently constituted intellect. Far from sharing such views, Thomas Aquinas expressly teaches that what is true to us cannot fail to be true even to God.

It could not be otherwise, since the principles of human knowledge are part and parcel of divine wisdom. A curious passage of Thomas' commentary on the Book of Job confirms this interpretation of the doctrine. Thomas is there reaching the point where Job, goaded into exasperation by the reproaches of his talkative friends, suddenly exclaims: "Shut up! Shut up! Let me say something! I want to speak to the Almighty; I want to argue my case with God" (Job 13:3). Whereupon Thomas Aquinas starts wondering: Is not this rather unseemly? A disputation between a man and God does not look right because of the inequality between the parties. But Thomas goes on to say, "It should be remembered that truth does not vary according to persons; when what a man says, is true, he is invincible, whomsoever he may be disputing with." [8]

To be sure, Job was aware of his own righteousness; he felt comforted by the gifts of wisdom and of science, but to him the main point was that he knew that what he had to say was true, God or no God. Don't browbeat me, Job tells God, and I shall not be afraid of disputing with thee: *non timebo tecum disputare*. Only speak to me and I shall answer, or else I surely shall speak and thou wilt answer me: *aut certe loquar et tu respondebis mihi*. To be true disciples of Thomas Aquinas, we would first have to put so much trust in the natural light of reason that nothing could make us doubt it, not even God.

Let us now look at the other side of the picture, for Thomas everywhere assents to the truth of Scripture, and this sort of assent has nothing to do with the evidence of reason; on the contrary, faith assents to the word of God in spite of the fact that reason does not clearly see it to be true. Thomas Aquinas was fully aware of the difference. At the very beginning of his career, in his commentary on the *Sentences* of Peter Lombard, as he was establishing the scientific nature of theology, he addressed to himself the well known objection: how can the theologian be wholly certain of his conclusions, since they hang on premises of which at least one is not known to be true in the light of reason, but is held on the strength of faith?

To the assertion that the theologian is not fully certain of his conclusions, Thomas answers that that is not true: *dicimus quod falsum est*. And passing straightway to the limit, Thomas adds this remark, almost unbelievable after what he has said about the evidence of the first principles: the believer assents to the truth of faith even more, and more firmly, than to the first principles of reason: *magis enim fidelis est et firmius assentit his quae sunt fidei quam etiam primis principiis rationis.*[9] In other words, the true believer is more certain of the dogma of the Trinity, for instance, than of the principle that one and the same thing cannot be at the same time itself and something else. So the believer assents more confidently to a proposition he does not *know* to be true, than to the propositions of which the truth is evident to him in the natural light of reason. This does not imply any doubt in his mind about the absolute validity of the first principles; what is at stake here is not the truth of those propositions but, quite precisely, the firmness of our assent to them.

Now, in the case of the first principles, we assent to the evidence of the natural light of a human, created, and finite mind, whereas faith is an assent of the intellect and heart to the truthfulness of the word of God. We are here reaching key positions of which every Christian is bound to know something, but which are seldom grasped in the fullness of their implications. They all are related to faith, a very simple thing indeed, since every Christian can make an act of faith, but an exceedingly complex notion and, at any rate, an often misunderstood one.

A first point is that religious faith never assents to anything except for one single reason, to wit, because God has revealed it. There are always reasons to believe, but such reasons are never sufficient to cause the assent of the believer to the proposition he believes; otherwise he would not believe its truth, he would know it.

A second point, which is the foundation of the whole theology of faith, is that the proper object of revelation of itself and in itself is always something man needs to know in order to achieve salvation in beatitude. There is such a distance from God to man that if we were left to our own resources, we could never bridge the ontological gap. Revelation precisely instructs us of what we need to know in order to attain an end far exceeding our natural means. This is so essential a notion that it could almost serve as a definition of the object of faith, namely, "that through which man attains beatitude." [10] The notion is simple; the trouble is that, along with what belongs to the object of faith properly and by itself, many other things are included in it indirectly and incidentally; most of the difficulties that beset the doctrine, at least in the mind of its readers, originate in that fact.

In discussing or interpreting these matters, we refer to *philosophy* and *theology*, but Thomas himself seldom uses the word "theology." True enough, we find it in the very title of the *Summa theologiae*, and for a good reason. Written for the use of students in faculties of theology, the work could bear no other title, but it was an ambiguous one because the word "theology" had long been used by the philosophers, especially by Aristotle, to point to the crowning part of metaphysics and therefore of philosophy.[11]

Now the kind of theology Thomas intends to teach has nothing in common with the philosophical knowledge of God, except its object. The two theologies are about God, hence their name, but their respective ways of knowing that same object are widely different. In order to mark the distinction, we ourselves now call "natural theology" the theology of the philosophers, and "revealed theology" the doctrine taught by the men we call theologians; Thomas himself does not use those expressions, and the better to avoid ambiguity, he calls theology *sacra doctrina*. Comparing it with the theologies of the philosophers, such as Plato, Aristotle, Proclus and others, Thomas says that there is between them and "sacred doctrine" a wider difference than is to be found between a species and another species within one and the same genus; they differ as one genus from another genus. *Differt secundum genus,* Thomas says of sacred doctrine as developed in his *Summa.*[12]

And indeed it is wholly distinct from the metaphysical knowledge of God, for the theology of the philosophers is the cognition of God such as man can obtain it; it is their own cognition of God, born of the human mind and limited to what we can know of God from our knowledge of his creatures. The theology of the philosophers belongs to the order of the things that are of this world and are, in the proper acceptation of the word, profane. Unlike that nonsacred theology, *sacra doctrina* proceeds from God; it imparts to us something of God's own self-knowledge so that through faith there is in us a finite and participated creation of the literally divine knowledge God has of himself. Because it proceeds from God, the sacred doctrine is in us something essentially divine. Faith is God already with us. Of course, the philosophical cognition of God is in itself an excellent thing, only it is a purely natural knowledge. The kind of information man naturally acquires about God, leaves us completely out of the inner life of the divinity.

Such is the meaning of the word "supernatural."

It points to the divine order which as such distinguishes the *secundum genus* from the natural order. There is no passing from the natural to the supernatural, but the supernatural can come down to inform the natural and to perfect it. Revelation does precisely that with respect to man's natural cognition of God. It divinizes it.

Being a participation in the knowledge God has of himself, faith already is, by mode of cognition, a substantial possession of God. Hence the classical doctrine of Scripture, followed by Thomas as well as by all Catholic theologians, that faith is *the substance of things to be hoped for* (Heb. 11:1). As Thomas understands them, these words signify "the relation of the act of faith to its end," which is God. Faith is said to be the substance of the things to be hoped for because it is the beginning of those very things, already possessed by the assent of the act of faith in which all are virtually included.[13]

Its essential relation to beatitude, then, is what radically distinguishes sacred doctrine from a mere philosophical knowledge of God. It is not simply information about God, it is an invitation from God to man; unless we accept that divine invitation, no beatitude is possible. Now the act of the virtue of faith is our acceptance of it; in the words of Scripture, *sine fide impossibile est placere Deo* (Heb. 11:6): without faith it is impossible to please God. To which the Epistle presently adds that he who wants to approach God (not merely to know about him) must believe that He exists and that He rewards those who seek Him: *Credere oportet accedentum ad Deum quia est, et quod inquirentibus se remunerator est*. Thomas Aquinas has made that doctrine his own.[14] Philosophy avails nothing to salvation; faith is its very beginning.

Such is the concrete situation with which Thomas in concerned. Most of our own controversies are inspired by a different spirit. Instead of dealing with the actual condition of man with respect to salvation, we focus our attention on the definition of abstract terms such as philosophy and theology, faith and reason. It is legitimate, even necessary, to do so. Thomas himself is careful to introduce such distinctions to clear up the meaning of terms around which certain discussions revolve, but the notions at stake interest him only to the extent that they help him to understand the complex structure of reality.

In the present case, one fact dominates the whole discussion: that it is the free decision of God, in creating the universe, to elevate man to perfect beatitude. Such a beatitude can only be found in the vision of God face to face, and since that vision exceeds the natural power of the human mind, God must reveal what man needs to know in order to be saved.

But that is not the whole question. Granting that at least some of the cognitions required for man's salvation are accessible to the natural light of reason, how many men in fact will be able to acquire them? This amounts to asking: how many men are there who enjoy the natural gifts of intellect, the moral qualities of will, and the leisure and social privileges without which a life successfully dedicated to metaphysical inquiry is practically impossible? This is one of those questions on which differences of opinion can be expected, but Thomas himself was far from entertaining an optimistic view of the situation.

According to him, metaphysicians are rare; there are few of them (*pauci*), indeed very few, (*paucissimi*).[15] Whatever their number, since God wanted the saving knowledge to be at the disposal of all men, he freely decided to reveal to them, not the whole of philosophy to be sure, nor even the whole of metaphysical truth, but at least those conclusions of natural theology which exceed the grasp, not indeed of the human mind, but of many human minds.

Such is the situation we are in. While the professors are painstakingly explaining that we cannot simultaneously know the truth of a proposition and believe it, God simply reveals the whole saving truth to all men so that even those who are not able to discover it by means of reason will nevertheless be able to hold it by faith. So we have to make our own choice—either to analyze the component elements of the situation or to envisage the situation itself and what it pleased God to do about it.

From this second point of view, which is that of theologian Thomas Aquinas, it is a fact that a certain amount of philosophically knowable truth has been revealed to man. God did not reveal it as philosophy; in Scripture there are no metaphysical demonstrations of the existence of God, of his oneness, of his providence, or even of the immortality of the soul. In short, Scripture contains no metaphysics at all, but it does contain —or imply—positive information on points of metaphysical interest. Given the complexity of the data,[16] a practically infinite variety of individual situations are likely to arise. Their detail escapes prevision, but the theologian must at least account for their very possibility.

Thomas Aquinas does more than foresee this; his own theology is calculated to include the totality of saving truth in all its forms and whatever its origin. What of it can be believed only, such as the mysteries of the Trinity and the Incarnation, will be taught as such; as to the parts of it that can be philosophically known, they will be received, first as revealed, since theological knowledge is at stake, then as philosophically justifiable in the light of reason. What is going to happen? The theologian does not know, nor does he need to know. Some of his readers will believe, others will try to know all that which they think they can know, still others will neither know nor believe. A phenomenological description of these concrete situations or at least of some of their general patterns, is a task which Thomas Aquinas left undone, because he was doing something else, but he has left directives to be observed in investigating such problems.[17]

Thus far, our discussion has been concerned with the meaning of two terms only, reason and faith, or philosophical knowledge and revelation. Such are the traditional data of the problem, but one term is missing, and its absence is largely responsible for the failure of those who discuss it to find a satisfactory answer to the question.

As was said, revelation is an invitation. What God reveals to be believed is what man needs to know in order to obtain eternal life. Since eternal life is the sovereign good and since by faith in revelation man holds a promise of it, the truth of faith is itself part of that good. As such this truth is an object of love as much as of cognition. He who is aware of holding in the object of his faith the very substance of the things to be hoped for—and finally the First Truth, God himself—is bound to love this object with his will at the same time that he knows it by his understanding. That is also why the understanding assents to truths it fails to see clearly and is unable to demonstrate. Such truths are beyond the grasp of cognition, not of love.

It is truly said that Thomism essentially is an intellectualism, but it is many other things, if only because in it the will is the prime mover of all the other powers of the soul.[18] This is particularly true in acts of the virtue of faith. Because intellectual evidence is lacking, "the intellect assents to matters of faith at the command of the will,"[19] and the will itself is directed to the object of faith as its own good, which is the vision of God.[20] The act of faith remains inexplicable if one omits to say that at the same time that God is infusing in the intellect the knowledge of the First Truth, he likewise infuses in the will, as a moving force, the grace of loving it. A participation in the love by which God eternally loves himself, the love in us of the object of revelation: this is charity. Because it quickens faith and prompts it to elicit its acts, the theologians say that the form of faith is—charity.[21]

From this conclusion as from a vantage point, the whole doctrine is seen in its full intelligibility.

And not only the personal doctrine of Thomas Aquinas, but the whole Augustino-Anselmian tradition as well. Why should faith seek understanding, if not because the understanding of faith is a halfway house on the road from plain faith to the beatific vision? Thomas Aquinas is not speaking of philosophy as it can be found in the mind of an unbeliever. Himself a theologian, living in the thirteenth century after Christ, Thomas speaks of the philosophizing reason of baptized men.

Now, of such men Thomas Aquinas says that their faith, so far as it is in its power, sufficiently inclines them to assent not only to all that is of faith essentially and absolutely, but also to all that precedes faith, accompanies it or follows it.[22] This statement covers a very wide field and we are far from the kind of classroom Thomism in which philosophical reason jealously protects its integrity against all religious influences. On the contrary, "when the will of a man is willing to believe, he loves the truth he believes, he turns it over in his mind (*super ea excogitat*) and if he can find reasons for it, he makes them his. And in this too reason does not exclude the merit of faith, but, rather, one should see in it the sign of a greater merit."[23]

Such is the climate in which Thomas Aquinas has always philosophized. There are other ways to philosophize, if only for the simple reason that there have been, still are, and always will be philosophies unrelated to Christian revelation. The man for whom Thomas Aquinas reserved his greatest philosophical admiration, Aristotle, had developed a philosophy entirely free from all religious influences, and of course Thomas was well aware of this fact, but it had nothing to do with his own personal problem. For he at least was a Christian, and the question for him was, could he himself philosophize as though he had never heard of the Christian revelation? Of course he could not. If a Christian undertakes to speak of God, how can he presume to neglect revelation, which is not a merely human knowledge of God, but a certain participation in the knowledge that God has of himself and an assimilation of the divine knowledge inasmuch as by infused faith we adhere to the First Truth itself for its own sake.[24]

Whenever I attempt to define the spirit of Thomas Aquinas' doctrine, I find myself confronted with a sort of antinomy, and so I start wondering what kind of man he was. In order to teach such a doctrine, he had to entertain an unqualified confidence in the aptitude of human reason to know scientific and philosophical truth; at the same time, he had to entertain an equally absolute confidence in the truth of the divine revelation as received by faith. Last, not the least, he must have been a man who could do both at one and the same time.

Unless we too begin to share in that twofold certitude, we cannot hope to participate in the true spirit of Thomism. Personal dispositions are at stake here, and they defy analysis, but ideas are also involved. Only a certain notion of the world, of man's place in the world, and of man's destiny, can provide a justification for such an attitude. We shall now proceed to an analysis of that notion.

CHAPTER II

The Master Plan of Creation

LET US START from our preceding conclusion, as formulated by Thomas Aquinas: metaphysics itself in its entirety is ordained to the knowledge of God as its ultimate end.[1] Seen in that perspective most of the philosophical statements of Saint Thomas acquire order and unity. And indeed, since man is an intelligent being in an intelligible universe, everything proceeds as though the reason for the existence of both was to make possible the cognition of God by some intellects. This is the point I shall attempt to make in this lecture, because to envisage man and the world from that vantage point is, I believe, to see them as nearly as possible as they were seen by Saint Thomas Aquinas.

God was entirely free to create the world or not to create it. But precisely because creation was not necessary, there must have been for God some reason to create. Moreover, God was free to create this world as we know it, or to create a different one; there again liberty presided over the divine operation, and since God was free to create whatever world he chose to, there must have been some reason, or motive, for him to create the very world we are in rather than another one. We must look for that reason in the nature of man and in the structure of the world.

Man is an intellectual substance. He is not the only one of his kind. In the language of Saint Thomas such substances are twofold in kind—the *spiritual substances,* or angels, and the *intellectual substances,* or men. The angels are called spiritual substances because, being bodiless, they are pure spirits; they do not *have* an intellect, they *are* one. Men are made of souls and bodies, so one cannot say of them that they *are* intellects, but, rather, that they *have* one. For that very reason they are called intellectual substances rather than intellects, or spirits.

From the intellectual substances to the spiritual substances the distance is considerable, yet it is a small one as compared with the distance there is from man to brute. For times like our own, when idealism is flourishing, it was a wise move to warn us against the temptation of what was called "angelism." But man is much farther removed from beasts than from angels. Saint Augustine was fond of quoting the words of Scripture (Ps. 8:6; Heb. 2:7): *minuisti eum paulo minus ab angelis:* Thou didst not make men much inferior to angels. As for Thomas Aquinas, in his *Contra gentiles* he regularly considers the spiritual creatures in general as forming one single genus in which two species are comprised, the angels and men. Their common feature is the intellect, which the angels are and men have. Despite this important difference, their intellectuality makes them equally immortal and equally able to be aware of their own existence, to reflect upon their knowledge and to direct their operations toward the same end, which is the vision of God.

The key to the meaning of the doctrine is the image of God in man. A biblical and a thoroughly religious notion indeed, since it is found in Genesis 1:26, where God himself says: *Let us make man to our own image and likeness.* At the same time, since the aim and scope of theology are to achieve some understanding of faith, Thomas asks himself: What is an image? This is a philosophical question. And his answer is, that to be an image is to resemble a model as closely as possible. Now all beings resemble God in that they are; some of them resemble God in that they live, and, finally, some resemble God in that they know by means of intellect and reason. These bear to

God the closest resemblance of all, so they are said to bear his image in their very being and to that extent they belong, so to speak, in a species similar to that of the divinity.

Of course, Thomas does not mean to say that God is included in a species and that man belongs in the same species as God, but he does say that there is in man a quality that makes him eminently similar to God, and it is understanding, or mind. The angels bear the same likeness to God, and for the same reason. So, along with man the angels communicate with God by a certain common quality which makes them resemble him. And that is what it is to be an image of God.

This is something Thomas himself does not find easy to express, but if you go to the trouble of reading the relevant passages in the *Summa theologiae* you will find that he does not hesitate to speak of man as being in the image of God because, in man's capacity as a rational creature, he somehow achieves a representation of God at the level of the species: *creaturae rationales videntur quodammodo ad repraesentationem speciei pertingere . . .* Again: *ad rationem imaginis pertinet aliqualis repraesentatio speciei.* Man represents the kind of being God is, because like God he too is an intelligent being. To be in God's image implies a resemblance of that sort and in that degree: *Imago importat similitudinem ut-*

cumque pertinentem ad speciei repraesentationem. In short, the qualitative unity created by the fact that some beings are intellects, or minds, is the cause that makes them so closely similar.[2]

What such natures are can be known from their operations, and their operations themselves are known from their ends. By ordaining the whole of human knowledge to the cognition of God, the philosophers have unwittingly revealed the nature of man's end. Whether or not angels and men are naturally able fully to reach their end is another question. The point is that such in fact is their end and that they are able to reach it, at least up to a point.

An intelligent being, man finds himself placed in a universe which he naturally desires to know, and of which the structure is such that, by investigating it on the basis of sense experience, the human reason finds itself conducted through a series of hierarchically ordered causes up to a supreme cause, which we call God. In the last analysis, the reason metaphysical knowledge is almost totally ordered to the cognition of God is that, in fact, the end of nature is to make God knowable to man and the end of man is, through knowing nature, to know Him.[3]

The relationship of reason and faith is therefore conditioned by that of nature and grace. The philosopher ascends from the knowledge of nature

to the knowledge of God, the theologian descends
from the perfections of God to those of his effects,
but since that twofold movement takes place
within one and the same mind, the philosopher
and the theologian are bound to meet.

It is quite possible to philosophize apart from
all revelation. The great philosophers of Greece
have done it, and some did it very well.[4] It remains possible to philosophize in the same way,
and it always will be possible; still, as a theologian, Thomas Aquinas considers it his duty to
avail himself of the whole truth accessible to man,
whatever its origin. That decision in a sense im-
poses limitations on his philosophical investiga-
tions. In his *Summa contra gentiles*, Thomas
twice states that he intends to philosophize so
far as the truth of faith is concerned: *quantum ad
fidei pertinet veritatem* (II, 5); *quantum ad fidei
veritatem pertinet* (II, 46, 1).

On the other hand, one is astonished to see
how extensively the truth of faith is concerned
with philosophy. If we take Thomas at his word,
the whole subject matter of the first three books
of the *Contra gentiles* falls within the domain
that philosophical speculation is competent to
handle. He expressly restates that view of his own
work at the beginning of Book IV (ch. 1, par. 5)
where he describes the first kind of knowledge of

things divine as that "in which natural reason can arrive at the knowledge of things divine through creatures." Only in the fourth book does he proceed to the things about God which surpass reason and can only be believed (par. 11). However, a mere glance at the contents of the first three books is enough to show how wide the jurisdiction of natural reason is in the doctrine of Thomas Aquinas; it extends beyond the frontiers of philosophy properly so called to all the parts of the revealed truth for which reason can find a satisfactory justification.[5]

Inversely, all the problems discussed in the fourth part of the work are handled, not indeed as philosophical problems, but in the language of the philosophers. Thomas is equally clear on his motive for doing so, and once more it is that, although philosophy ascends to the knowledge of God through creatures while sacred doctrine grounded in faith descends from God to man by the divine revelation, *the way up and the way down are the same.* Hence, Thomas concludes, "we must proceed in the same way in the things above reason which are believed, as we proceeded in the foregoing with the investigation of God by reason." There is not one world for revelation and another one for reason; because the whole reality has God for its only cause, it is one world, and although we must follow two generically different lights in investigating it, since reason too is one, it proceeds in both cases in the same way.[6]

The *Contra gentiles* is the work in which the view of the world proper to Thomas Aquinas reveals itself in its perfect unity. It is the most personal of his works; never taught and probably unfit for classroom consumption, it is the nearest equivalent of what a properly Thomistic philosophy would be. It contains all that reason can say to prove what can be proved in sacred doctrine, and it also establishes that whatever reason cannot prove in that doctrine at least contains no rational impossibilities. The work is theological from beginning to end, but in it scholastic theology at its best achieves a unified view of the universe, of its cause and of its end under the converging lights of reason and revelation.

The second and third books of the *Contra gentiles* represent the very core of a rational interpretation of the Christian world. Thomas discloses there what seems to have been to him, so to speak, the master plan of creation. Why did God create a world, and precisely this world that we know? Only a careful investigation of its structure can suggest an intelligent answer to that question.

The universe is an ordered whole, a hierarchy of beings, and although each particular being is good in itself, their general order is better still, since it includes, over and above the perfection of each individual thing, that of the whole.[7] Now the key to that order, as Thomas sees it, is that "it was required for the perfection of the universe that there should be in it some intellectual natures."[8] More precisely, it was required that "certain intellectual creatures should occupy the summit of creation."[9]

In a first superficial sense this seems to mean that intellectuality is the finest flower and ornament of the universe, but Thomas means more than that. If it contained no intellectual creatures, the world would not make sense. Today, some existentialists display great acumen in explaining that the very core of this universe—is absurdity. Thomas certainly sees things differently, but he might well grant at least that there is no other choice. The world is either fundamentally intelligible or fundamentally absurd. It is intelligible if all the other beings in it are there in view of the intellectual ones, and if, in turn, the intellectual ones are there in view of knowing God; otherwise it should be granted that the world does not make sense. Without intellectual creatures creation would be a meaningless act of God.

Let us try to make this clear. The only intelligible motive for the creation of the world is the goodness of God and his desire to communicate it by producing beings similar to himself. Now an effect that resembles its cause imitates it; when the cause is God, all that the effect can do is to share in his perfection by imitating his goodness, as far as can be done short of being God. All effects somehow imitate and resemble their causes, but we know that resemblance to their cause is particularly close in the case of the intellectual substances, which God made in his own image. For an intellect to know a thing is, so to speak, to become that very thing by mode of representation. The thing I know becomes myself by my cognition of it, unless we prefer to say that I am becoming it through knowing it. Hence this first conclusion: "Since only an intellect can know the divine goodness," and since to know this goodness was the only way for the universe to share perfectly in the goodness of its cause, "there had to be intellectual creatures in the world." [10]

How close their likeness to God is, can be judged from another remark of Thomas Aquinas: "Man is united by mode of likeness with higher substances, since of all the operations of man, intellection alone is found also in separate substances and in God." [11] God is the self-subsisting thought, angels are separate intelligences, man too is endowed with an intellect, and after man the intellectual light seems to disappear from the great chain of being. No wonder then that Thomas Aquinas called man "such a noble creature."

We don't know if, even apart from angels, there are in the world other creatures more or less like man, but if they are more noble than man, we can be sure it is because they are more intelligent.

In the light of that conclusion, the structure of the universe assumes its full intelligibility. We say that God is the ultimate end of man, but He is the ultimate end of all things. How could it be otherwise? God is the supreme being, and since being is good, God also is the sovereign good. And since good is desirable *qua* good, the supreme good necessarily is the end in view of which all things operate.

Lastly, since the other causes operate only in order to reach some end, their final cause also is the first and highest of all causes: "The ultimate end therefore is the first of all causes. Now to be the first cause necessarily belongs to the first being, who is God . . . So God is the ultimate end of all things." [12] This is straight philosophical reasoning; in fact, it is the doctrine common to several philosophers before and after the time of Thomas Aquinas. Plato, Aristotle, Descartes, Leibnitz and many others have upheld that same view on purely philosophical grounds. And yet, once more, in another style and in an altogether different light we find it taught in Holy Writ: *Ego sum Alpha et Omega, the First and the Last.*[13] The same truth, known at unequal degrees of depth, is here coming to man from different sources. Once engaged on that road, Thomas will follow it to the end.

Perhaps the best known introduction to the spiritual life is the *De imitatione Christi;* in a sense, the whole cosmology of Thomas Aquinas could have for its title, *De imitatione Dei.* For indeed, a certain inborn desire to imitate God and to emulate his perfection is the secret which even the physical universe is revealing in its existence as well as in its natural operations. God is, and creatures are. God creates, and they cause, for though to cause is not to produce being from nothingness, it nevertheless is to produce such and such being. So already from the lowest level of inorganic substance—the rock, the mineral, even their physicochemical elements—everything tends to imitate God by being, by striving to continue to be, and by becoming for other things the cause of their existence: "Every thing tends toward the divine likeness inasmuch as it tends to be the cause of other things." [14]

True of all creatures inasmuch as they are, this is even more true of living beings inasmuch as they live, and it is eminently true of those that are endowed with intellectual knowledge. The merely natural beings are not aware of the physical love that prompts them to operate. Their very operation is, in fact, their desire. Intellectual beings, such as man, are able to reflect upon their activity and to realize its motives. They do know that to be a cause is to imitate the divine causality. For such beings, to cause is more than merely to resemble God, it is to cooperate with him and, in a way, to help him. At least that is what Scripture says (1 Cor. 3:9): *Dei sumus adjutores;* and Dionysius insists that "of all things, to become a co-worker with God is the more divine." [15]

Instead of being unconscious desires of God— as the merely material causes are—intellectual substances imitate the free, intelligent causality of God, and in a sense they are collaborating with it. Only such causes can initiate series of causal operations; they are the only true principal causes, all the others being instrumental ones. When reflection follows any series of causes and effects till it reaches a principal one, it always stops at a living and knowing cause. In short, behind each and every operation of nature an intellectual substance is at work: *quodlibet opus naturae est opus substantiae intelligentis.* [16]

This should help us understand the notion, widely controverted yet so simple, of the natural desire of God.

Even among those who consider themselves Thomists, many theologians either reject that doctrine or else minimize it to the point of emptying it of all meaning. They are afraid of it because it seems to attribute to man what would amount to a natural knowledge of his supernatural end. In fact, it does nothing of the sort, but, were it otherwise, the doctrine of Thomas Aquinas is such that man would be the only being not to be prompted in what he is, does and makes, by a natural desire of God. As has been seen, all creatures are quickened by that desire. They all participate in God's likeness by performing their operations. The only difference with man is that, since he is an intellectual substance, his proper operation is intellectual knowledge, so that his proper way to become similar to God is to know him. In Thomas' own words, the end of every intellectual creature, angel or man, is to understand God by its intellect: *oportet quod hoc sit finis intellectualis creaturae, scilicet intelligere Deum.*[16]

Let us try to understand this correctly. Thomas does not say that man naturally knows that his ultimate end is to enjoy the vision of God face to face in eternal blessedness. This is the "good news" which the Gospel has revealed to men, and without that revelation they still would not know it. Thomas still less says that, once informed by God of his supernatural end, man is able to reach it naturally and by his own means. Thomas simply says that in point of fact the ultimate end of man does consist in the intellectual cognition of the first truth and therefore of the first cause, which is God.

Once more, Thomas is speaking here of intellectual substances in general, that is to say, in the first place, of the pure intelligences, or angels; but man too is an intellectual substance, even if one of the lowest rank, and that is the reason Thomas explicitly stipulates that "the end of every intellectual substance, even the lowest one (*finis cujuslibet substantiae intellectualis, etiam infimae*) is the intellectual knowledge of God." [17]

This is like a crossroads where the main themes of the doctrine seem to meet. For instance, it is because God made man in His image that to resemble God by knowing Him is the ultimate end of man; so the slightest information about Him is more precious to us than even the perfect scientific knowledge of nature.[18]

Again, this is the reason Aristotle and the other philosophers of old, who knew nothing of Christianity, used to call metaphysics the science of the divinity, *scientia divina*—because it is that part of philosophy through which the whole is ordained to God as its end. Is not this a sign that, revelation or no revelation, the knowledge of God is the ultimate goal of every human cognition and operation? Yes indeed, *est cognito divina finis ultimus omnis humanae cognitionis et operationis.*[19]

Again, and more deeply still, is not that desire of God the hidden force that drives the mind of philosophers through the whole encyclopedia of the sciences of nature, up to the consideration of the first cause? The long pilgrimage of the mind from mathematics, through physics and biology, to metaphysics, is a visible manifestation of a desire without which there would be neither metaphysics nor natural theology. To repeat, man naturally desires to know the first cause, just as he naturally desires to know the last end.[20] And so on, indefinitely: *est igitur ultimus finis hominis cognoscere Deum . . . ; est igitur ultimus finis hominis ipsa Dei cognitio . . .*

Thomas even sees a kind of acceleration in that pursuit of God by the mind; the more a man knows, the more his desire to know God increases, just as falling bodies accelerate as they get nearer to the ground. Here, as if in a desperate effort to make things as clear to others as they are to him, Thomas gathers together within one single sentence what is to him both the metaphysical conclusion of reason and the revealed certitude of faith: "The ultimate end of man, as well as of every intellectual substance, is called his felicity, or blessedness, because that is what every intellectual substance desires as its ultimate end and wills for its own sake; therefore, the ultimate happiness of every intellectual substance is to know God." In short, man's natural desire tends toward the most noble object of knowledge, and this is what Aristotle says in the tenth book of his *Nicomachean Ethics* (ch. 7), that "the ultimate felicity of man is speculative, consisting in the contemplation of the best there is to contemplate"; but it is also said in Matthew (5:8): "Blessed are the clean of heart, for they shall see God." [21]

Whether or not this doctrine is philosopically true and theologically correct certainly is a debatable point, since it has been so hotly debated. What cannot possibly be doubted is that it is the authentic doctrine of Saint Thomas Aquinas. It is true that Cajetan has done his very best to explain it away, but Thomas Aquinas, not Cajetan, is the Common Doctor of the Church. The very spirit of Thomism is at stake here. Let us remember the classical formula: "Grace does not destroy nature, but perfects it." [22]

Now the way grace perfects nature is clearly visible here. Because of its intellectual substances, the world presents a paradoxical situation. Of itself, an intellect is able to know any being whatever. According to the classical formula, its object is *ens in communi*, being in general, and since God is being, he is comprised in the object of the intellect. On the other hand, infinite being is unproportionable to finite intellects, so that in his capacity as an intellectual substance, man finds himself unable to completely reach his natural end. He can reach it somehow, for nature never is in vain, but even after forming in metaphysics an abstract notion of God, which is about the best he can do, man realizes that his philosophical knowledge falls far short of what a true cognition of God would be. In fact, truly to know God would be to see him. The greatest of the philosophers never envisaged the possibility of such a cognition, and rightly so, since in fact it is not naturally accessible to man. The good news of the Gospel precisely is that God has freely decided to provide man, through revelation and grace, with the means required for the fulfillment of his natural desire. For such is the secret paradox of all intellectual substance, that it is a finite power virtually capable of an infinite object.

And such also is the mystery of the natural desire of man to know God. The perfect good of man is to know God in some way or other. The quest of "so noble a nature" for knowledge and wisdom cannot be wholly in vain, for in the last analysis it is nothing other than man's quest for a more and more perfect cognition of God.[23]

The successive stages of that human epic are

described by Thomas Aquinas in a long chain of chapters of *Contra gentiles,* III, 26-40, where it is successively shown that man's felicity is neither pleasure, nor wealth, nor moral virtue, nor art, nor the common-sense knowledge of God, nor the sophisticated knowledge of him obtained through philosophy, nor even, as some have thought, the knowledge of pure spirits, superior to man but inferior to God. Great philosophers have tried all those answers, and they all felt that none of them was the perfect one. All this is not to Thomas an abstract dialectical deduction; rather, it is the moving story of the pilgrimage of humankind in its quest for the object of true beatitude, and its inability to find it.[24]

Sharing in the anxiety of the early philosophers, Thomas invites us to realize in what straits those geniuses found themselves; theirs was an anxiety from which we now are free since we know that true felicity can be had only after this life, when the saints are like the angels "who always see God in heaven" (Matt. 18:10). There is no better expression of the true spirit of Thomism, in which nature is preambulatory to grace. Philosophy, which is about nature, establishes the possibility of what revelation promises; revelation brings to man the certitude that the obscure aspirations of his nature will be fulfilled in eternity.

Some theologians reproach Thomism for attributing too much to nature at the expense of the supernatural order of grace; but they forget that Thomas sees God as the author of the two orders, who has created nature in view of grace. The true divine motive for creation precisely was the aptitude of certain natures to be supernaturalized. Only intellectual substances possess such natures, and this is the reason they have been created, for indeed nature in no way includes the supernatural order of grace, but it does include its possibility.

Reduced to its simplest technical expression, the central truth of Thomism as a *scholastic* theology, is this *natural possibility* of the supernatural order. Not, of course, the possibility that the natural order could elevate itself to grace—that would be an absurd supposition—but the possibility that nature can be elevated by God to the supernatural order of grace—in this case the contrary supposition is absurd. If, of itself, nature were not open to grace, even God could not perfect it by supernatural means. Even God could not cause man to see his creator face to face if man's nature were incapable of being raised to that state of perfection. But we know it can be, and the fact that we can infer it from a mere inspection of the human mind explains why Thomas includes his demonstration of the possibility of the beatific vision in the third book of *Contra gentiles* among the questions to which natural reason can find an answer.

For indeed natural reason cannot demonstrate that God has called mankind to eternal blessedness and granted us the means to attain it, but once informed by revelation that God has done so, philosophical reason can demonstrate that given the nature of the intellect and of its object, if it so pleases God, a beatifying vision of God is not an intrinsic impossibility. On the contrary, since the intellectual substances naturally desire to know God, to see him face to face is the complete satisfaction of that natural desire. This is what Thomas Aquinas himself says in one sentence of an almost frightening theological density: "Since it is impossible for a natural desire to be in vain, as would be the case if it were not possible to succeed in knowing the divine substance—a thing which all minds naturally desire to do—it is necessary to say that it is possible for the substance of God to be seen by the intellect, both that of the separate intellectual substances and that of our own souls." [25]

The whole theology of Thomas Aquinas rests upon this optimistic view of the created world and of man's destiny. By "optimistic" I do not intend to suggest that Thomas was of a cheerful temper. Perhaps he was, but that is something I do not know and, besides, I do not think he would have consulted his feelings in metaphysical matters. But he had a certain notion of God; he also had a very precise notion of the intellect, an immaterial power capable of knowledge because of its very immateriality, and, as such, of a nature not totally unlike that of God. True enough, the distance from man to God is infinite, but the essence of God's image is not infinitely different from that of God, as is the case with plants and brutes. Man and God would then be totally unlike, except inasmuch as both are beings.

In a sentence in which we find him struggling for words, Thomas says that the divine substance —far from being *wholly foreign* to the created intellect as, for instance, "sounds are to sight, or immaterial substances to sense knowledge"—is "the first intelligible and the principle of all intellectual cognition, but exceeding the power of the created intellect, as the extreme sensible qualities exceed the power of our senses." [26] All the intelligibles are cognate to all the intellects, even God, but just as too much light blinds the sight, too much intelligibility confuses the intellect.

There is a still deeper reason for the kind of metaphysical optimism that pervades the theology of Saint Thomas. Far from overlooking the presence of evil in the world, he asserts that creatures, not God, are responsible for it. In itself, being is good, and God is supremely good because he is being itself in its purity. In discussing the general design of creation, theologians like to stress the fact that apart from respecting their essences God had no obligation toward his creatures. From the point of view of his absolute power, God was free to shut man out of the kingdom of heaven or to open its gates to him. And that is true, but it is not the whole truth.

Had he not been given the graces necessary to salvation, man would have been victim of no injustice. He still would be, operate, and achieve a valuable degree of felicity by his natural knowledge of God. The essence of man, a finite intellectual substance, does not include the right to enjoy beatitude in the vision of the divinity. But when Thomas considers the general economy of creation, he cannot help wondering why God should have created intellectual substances, that is to say, creatures naturally anxious to know him, unless he intended to fulfill the natural desire he himself had implanted in their hearts by making them capable of intellectual knowledge. God is the end of all things as well as their principle.

The question then is not: *could* God have created man without making him able to enjoy the final vision of his creator? God can make anything that is not self-contradictory, and it certainly would not have been contradictory for him to

have created man without opening to him the
gates of heaven. In fact, not all men will see God.
The absolute power of God (*potentia Dei absoluta*) is not at stake here, for his all-powerfulness
never operates in a state of separation from his
wisdom (*potentia Dei ordinata*). Now, the point
of view of wisdom is that of the final cause; in
this case, we do know that God has created man
in His own image, an intellectual substance capable of knowing being as such and, by the same
token, anxious to know it. The obvious inference
is that our intellect was made for the purpose of
seeing God: *intellectus noster factus est ad hoc
quod videat Deum.*[27] Of course, even God could
not create a finite mind *naturally capable* of seeing infinite being. Only the divinely infused light
of glory can enable man fully to attain his *naturally desired* end.

Is not this a paradoxical conclusion? Certainly,
but in the first place, that which transcends nature
is always seen by nature as paradoxical, and God
assuredly transcends nature, being supernatural
by definition. Next, Thomas Aquinas is not erect-
ing a Christian theology on the foundation of an
Aristotelian philosophy but rather on the basis of
the Christian notion of man conceived as an intellectual substance created in the image of God.
As such, man is an acting and operating substance
created in view of its operation.[28] Like all other

created substances, man operates to reunite himself with his cause, to which he is indebted for his good as well as for his being. It so happens that man's cause escapes the grasp of any intellectual substance, angel or man; it is therefore evident that in the master plan of creation, God has eternally foreseen by his wisdom that such substances, created by his all-powerfulness, would have to be provided with the supernatural means to attain their end. In short, Thomism is a doctrine in which the human intellect naturally desires an end that it cannot attain by merely natural means.

There was a deep affinity between the Christian world of Thomas Aquinas and the pagan world of Aristotle,[29] yet they were different worlds. At any rate it cannot be doubted that the universe of the Common Doctor is such as I have described it. No end of quotations could be mustered to support that description. One of them can do for all, because it says all that Thomas has to say on the subject: "Although man has a natural inclination toward his ultimate end, he cannot attain it by natural means but by grace only, and this is because of the eminence of that very end."[30]

Propter eminentiam ipsius finis: only the transcendence of the Christian God is such that it has the power and the wisdom to create such an ontological gap, and to bridge it. This is true of angels above man,[31] and it is equally true of all beings below man; the difference is that the end of the natural desire of man, as an intellectual substance whose proper operation is to know, is to understand God.[32] Some will object—how could man naturally desire to see God if he is not naturally able to see him? Does not Aristotle say, and Thomas Aquinas repeat, that natural desire cannot possibly be frustrated? Yes, Thomas answers, but this precisely is the reason God's grace makes it possible for man to see him, notwithstanding the disproportion of man's nature to the end of his desire. Besides, it was proved above (ch. 50) that every intellect naturally desires the vision of the divine substance, but natural desire cannot be incapable of fulfillment. Therefore, any created intellect whatever can attain to the vision of the divine substance, and the inferiority of its nature is no impediment.[33]

To contain substances of which the highest natural desires can be fulfilled only by God using supernatural means is the characteristic feature of the Thomist universe. "Since the end of man is felicity, to which his natural desire tends, his felicity cannot be placed in something which man cannot attain, otherwise man would be in vain, and his natural desire would be in vain, which is impossible." [34] Such a universe was exactly what it had to be in order to account for the kind of speculation practiced by Saint Thomas Aquinas. It was all of a piece. Because in it nature was created in view of grace, man must both know and believe. By reason, man knows the universe and naturally desires to know its cause; by faith, he assents supernaturally to God's revelation; so *not merely to know* something about that cause, *but to see* it, is for man a possibility.[35] So nature fully makes sense in the light of grace, and rational knowledge in the light of faith.

After all, we might have guessed it—for how did Aristotle describe the ultimate felicity of man if not as "speculative in accord with the contemplation of the best object of speculation"? But what was the good news brought to man by the Gospel? *"Blessed are the clean of heart for they shall see God."* And, *"This is eternal life, that they may know Thee, the only true God."*[36] Now there is a reason for that admirable harmony of nature and grace. It is that their end is one and the same: the Lord has made all things because of himself: *Universa propter semetipsum operatus est Dominus* (Prov. 16:4).

But this is not yet the end of our inquiry. What is that being which God is and which all the rest strive to imitate? Unless we consider it in itself, we shall miss what is probably the keystone of

Thomism; for if, in it as in the world, the way to God and from God is the same—*est eadem via ascensus et descensus*—the reason is that in both cases the mind is moving between beings and Being.

CHAPTER III

A Metaphysics of the Name of God

THERE ARE DIFFERENT SCIENCES. Each one of them inquires into a different mode of being. Extended being for mathematics, being in motion for physics, living being for biology, thinking being for anthropology—there is a science for every mode of being. The use of the so-called human sciences has complicated the situation still more, since because of them the sciences of nature now cover all the activities of man, while in turn the psychology of man now includes an interpretation of all the sciences of nature, since man is part of nature and all the sciences are products of the human mind.

Despite their differences, however, the objects of the diverse sciences have something in common. Since all the objects are "modes of being," all the sciences are finally concerned with being.

Scientists as such are not interested in being. They take it for granted, and indeed, from their own point of view, rightly so. If there were nothing, there would be neither science nor scientists, so there would be no questions at all. The men who wonder about being are not the scientists, they are philosophers and, more precisely, the metaphysicians. That is their own question, the question which Aristotle already called the eternal object of all inquiries, present and past, the question perpetually asked and never satisfactorily answered: *ti to on?* (Metaph. X, 1, 1028b 2-7). What is being?

In the thirteenth century after Christ, when it reached Thomas Aquinas, the question had become considerably older, but it had not yet found its perfectly correct answer. Yet Thomas felt neither surprised nor downhearted. He knew that mankind advances in the discovery of truth (in his own word, *pedetentim*) step by step. He also knew that the long-sought-for truth was within reach. After looking for reality in the sensible qualities of beings, then in their essences, then in their substances, philosophy had finally realized that true reality is actual essence. At least twice Thomas Aquinas recounted this sixteen-century-long metaphysical epic,[1] and he entertained no doubt about its name.

It is better to be a plant than to be a stone,

because to be a plant is to be all that which a stone is, plus something which the stone is not. It is better to be an animal than to be a plant, for the same reason, and it is better to be a man than a brute. But to be is not merely better than all these things. It is better in an altogether different way: because it is the first and universal condition, without which there would be nothing else. When there is no being, there are neither minerals nor plants nor animals nor men; in short, there is nothing at all.

The more Thomas thought of that elementary truth, the more he was convinced the philosophers had been right. But perhaps they themselves did not know how right they were. Inasmuch as actual existence is a condition of all the rest, it stands alone as a frightening mystery at the core of reality. For if what I have just said is true, actual existence does not add up to the rest. That is why when my colleagues ask me how to teach metaphysics, I always answer, "I do not know." Because the first lecture will be about the object of metaphysics: it is being. And if your students ask you, What is being? they will be asking you a question which men have been asking for twenty-four centuries without finding the answer.

The reason why we do not find the answer is that actual existence is a perfection without which there is nothing, but which is not at all a perfection belonging to the same class as the other perfections. There is an old story, a popular story, in France, about the horse of the knight Roland. He was a wonderful horse; he had all possible characteristics, all possible qualities. He was fast, he was strong, he did not eat, he did not drink. He had only one defect. He was dead. But that is the question! To be, obviously, is a perfection. It is not merely one perfection—one more perfection in the same line as the other perfections; it is entirely different. How can we understand this? Very wisely, our students—and sometimes their professor—forget about it and get rid of the problem by that simple method.

But if we want to philosophize, it is really *the* problem of problems. In Thomas' technical language, actual existence, which he calls *esse*, is that by virtue of which a thing, which he calls *res*, is a being, an *ens*. It is the being-hood or being-ness of being. It is *be* in being. It is *to be* that makes a certain thing to be a being. *Esse* is defined by its essence, namely that which the thing is.[2]

The essence of man—to be a rational creature— is what makes a man the kind of being he is. The actual existence of a thing is that which causes it to be, and since apart from actual existence an essence is nothing, the act in virtue of which a thing is, or exists, is the supreme act of that thing.

In Thomas' own words, it is the perfection of all its perfections.[3] But actual existence (*esse*) does not perfect the other perfections by adding to them another one. It is the entirely different kind of perfection without which no other one can be. The uniqueness of this property of being already points out its particular affinity with God.

This thought was followed by another in the mind of Saint Thomas: precisely because it does not belong in the order of essence, the act of being has no quiddity of its own. Neither a thing, nor any intrinsic constituent of a thing as such, it cannot be conceived apart from the essence which it causes to be a being. We can form quidditative concepts of horse or of man and express them in the form of definitions, but because the act of being is not an essence, it cannot be conceived and defined in itself.

Existence can be signified. We signify it by a judgment, and here again the peculiar nature of existence can be observed in the very form of the judgment that signifies it. The judgments signifying the essences of things vary according to the diversity of those essences. The definition of man is not the same as that of horse, which itself differs from that of oak or of stone. On the contrary, the form of the judgment signifying actual existence is always the same. Whatever the nature of the thing, all we can say about its existence is: it is, or else it is not. That *whatness* of things differs according to their respective natures, but concerning their *thatness,* only one of two things can be done—it can be affirmed or denied.

A third and last observation that occurred to the mind of Thomas Aquinas was that in the case of actual existence the mode of cognition is not the same as it is when the question arises of knowing the essence, or the nature of the thing. When we are told what a certain thing is, our intellect is supposed to understand the meaning of its definition. It is all a question of understanding, or of comprehending certain notions.

Not so with existence. All we can do about it is to point it out and say: "it is here, it is there, it is gone." We ourselves know existence by seeing, touching or hearing it; and we can make it known to others by making them perceive it in some sensible experience. Of course, we often have reasons to affirm the existence of something we do not see nor perceive in any way; in this sense, existence can be demonstrated, but in such cases what the judgment affirms is that an experiential cognition of its objects is possible, or in other words that its object is of such a nature that its existence can be actually perceived. We do not see God, but we believe that, since he is, he can be seen in some sort of intellectual intuition.

The general consequence of those remarks is

that when one speaks of being, the object of one's discourse is a thing that has actual existence. Of its act of existence we know only that it is, and we grasp it only as given in the thing that it causes to be. It itself is not a being but rather is that which makes such and such a thing to be a being. In Thomas' own terse words: "The whole substance is that which is, and the *esse* itself (to be) is that on account of which the substance is called a being."[4]

That was a common sense view of reality, for everybody realizes that since actual existence is the perfection that makes all the other perfections possible, it also is a perfection different in kind from all the other ones. To posit the existence of a being is to posit at once as real all the qualities included in its definition; to take away existence is not merely to deprive that being of one of its attributes, it is to suppress them all at one fell stroke.

As is always the case, metaphysics does nothing more here than to take common sense seriously. The metaphysician is prompted by a sort of innate conviction that common sense, though often wrong about superficial aspects of reality that are distorted by sensory illusions, is usually right when it comes to fundamental intuitions concerning the very essence of reality. Common sense is not metaphysical knowledge. Mainly practical in its object, it contents itself with drawing at once from given situations the sensible rules of conduct they suggest. In the case of being, common sense would sum up all the preceding philosophical reflections in some simple sentence, such as: Don't give that thing another thought: *it does not exist.*

The philosopher's attitude is quite different at least in this: to him, actual existence always deserves to be given another thought. To Thomas Aquinas it did not look right to dismiss as unimportant that without which nothing else would be. Hence, in Thomas' own philosophical view of the world, the often restated conviction that, beyond all the other properties of any being and so to speak at the very core of reality, there is a sort of static energy [5] in virtue of which the being actually is, or exists. Since this "energy" is not a "thing," it cannot be defined, but we know it from its effect, which is actual existence, and we also know it as the condition for the possibility of all the rest.

There always is something arresting and enigmatic about what Thomas says of the verb *to be,* especially of its infinitive which he uses as a substantive, *esse.* It is something "fixed and at rest in being": *esse est aliquid fixum et quietum in ente.*[6] Static as it is, since it is innocent of all becoming, "to be" nevertheless is a power of an active kind; it is a power of being: *virtus essendi.*[7]

It is the very act in virtue of which the thing exists: *unumquodque est per suum esse.*[8] The act whereby each thing actually is, is its own, so that there is one act of being for each particular being: *non idem est esse hominis et equi, nec hujus hominis et illius hominis.*[9] In short, the "to be" of a being is its very core, that which is most intimate in it, and in this we find the justification of what was said above, that it is, in each particular thing, the actuality of all its acts and the perfection of all its perfections: *Esse est actualitas omnium actuum et propter hoc est perfectio omnium perfectionum.*[10]

And now, let us brace ourselves for a metaphysical shock. Thomas says in one of his earliest works that God is innermost in each and every thing, just as its own *esse* is innermost in the thing: *Deus est unicuique intimus, sicut esse proprium rei est intimum ipsi rei.*[11]

A rather startling statement indeed, and one I do not advise you to repeat without first specifying that Thomas himself is speaking. You would probably be charged with pantheism. But Thomas Aquinas was not a particularly safe Thomist; rather than safe, he preferred to be right, which is not the same thing. The safe Thomist prefers not to state the whole truth if asserting it without qualification would risk misleading his readers. Thomas proceeds differently. Having first made

sure of the truth, he states it as forcibly as possible; after all, if his meaning is clear, those who
misinterpret it are responsible for their own errors.[12] In the present case, Thomas means that
God is present in all beings because he is their
cause; so he is in them as the cause is in its effect.

A simple comparison will show the meaning of
the doctrine. Let us imagine a violinist who is
performing a solo sonata of Bach. We do not think
that the being of the sounds produced by his art
is the artist's own being. The proof of it is that
the sonata can be recorded and kept separately
so that it will subsist independently of the person
of its performer. Still, while it is being performed,
the sonata owes its whole existence to the violinist; it *is*, but only in virtue of the being of the
artist. It participates in that being as effects participate in their causes, that is, by deriving their
being from that of their causes. Nor is this an idle
metaphor. Man or bird, when the singer ceases to
sing, the song ceases to be; the being of the cause
really is *in* the effect.

This is exactly what Thomas Aquinas intends
to say: "God is said to be in each and every thing,
inasmuch as he gives to things their own being
and nature." [13] Now God did not simply give being
to creatures at the moment of creation, he is giv-
ing it to them all the time; by a simple, undivided
act, he incessantly causes the world to be, so that

if he withdrew his support from his creation, the whole thing would at once cease to be, as the song of the singer who stops singing. Do we realize that our whole being—and first of all its actual existence—hangs on the intimate presence of God? We should. If we did, we would also realize that in true Thomism, metaphysics and theology are by the same token spirituality and piety.

Let us draw these conclusions together. The core of reality, beyond its matter, its forms, and the substances that arise from their union, is the very act in virtue of which a thing is a being. God is present in each and every thing as the cause is in its effect, by imparting to it actual existence. The conclusion is that God is present in the totality of all the elements of which the substances consist, as well as in all their operations, from the mere fact that he is present in the act of *esse* owing to which they are. But since effects always witness to the presence of their causes, it should be possible for us, starting from beings, to form some notion of the very nature of their cause.

Now all the proofs of God's existence, whatever their number and their formulation, end in positing him as the cause of the world. It is therefore necessary to think of God as of an ultimate and pure act of being, or better still, as of *esse* itself in its absolute purity: *ipsum purum esse*. All the other beings are essences, or substances that *have* their respective acts of being; but their universal cause is not an essence having such an act, it *is* that very act. Thomas never tires of affirming and reaffirming this: "the divine *esse* is to itself its own essence or nature";[14] "the divine substance is *esse* itself";[15] "and that, namely *to be* in act, is the divine essence itself";[16] "the *esse* of God is his substance," [17] and so on, so to speak, indefinitely.

In the mind of Saint Thomas this metaphysical conclusion followed from a rational analysis of the structure of reality. It came at the end of long historical development in the course of which, after successively identifying being with individual being and then with substantial being—at the end of a sixteen-century-long evolution—the human mind had reached the conclusion that beyond what makes beings individuals and then substances, one must first posit the ontological energy that causes them to be.

As to the cause of all those causes, it could be nothing other than the very act of being, taken in its purity. Thomas was not including himself in that history. Of the philosophers whom he mentioned by name, not one had been a Christian or a theologian, and yet, for the third time, we find ourselves confronted with one of those unexpected harmonies of nature and grace, of philosophy and theology, of reason and revelation which seem to be of the very essence of Thomism. For indeed, while philosophy concludes that the first cause is the very act of being in its purity—*ipsum esse*—revelation teaches us, in Exodus 3:14, that the proper name of God is WHO IS, or *QUI EST*, because it is exclusively proper to him to be nothing other than his own *esse*, his own act of being.[18]

However, I can only say these things in words; it takes a certain personal familiarity with the thought of Thomas Aquinas himself to see these things and, so to speak, to touch them. Such an intimate blending of metaphysical reasoning and of religious faith in revelation is extraordinary indeed. Some doubt its sincerity; others feel scandalized by it, and yet the true spirit of Thomism is to find in it a source of wonder and joy for the soul as well as for the mind.

The whole perfection of God is contained in his *esse*. So it will suffice to form a notion of his *esse* in order to know the being of God. But there are difficulties. The fundamental one is connected with the very nature of man as a knowing being. An intellectual substance, but not a spiritual one (a pure "spirit"), man derives his knowledge from sensation. Give him objects to see, to touch, or to perceive by any one of his sense organs, and he will have something to know. His intellect then sets to work and abstracts from the data of sense a general notion applicable to all the objects that belong to the same species as the particular ones he is experiencing. As Thomas bluntly puts it: "the intellect needs a body for its object." [19]

Since by definition metaphysics (trans-physics) is about nonphysical objects, one cannot hope to derive from it the same kind of satisfaction as from the study of physics, for instance, or from any other science of observation. Because of its very nature the intellect feels at home in all the sciences that consist of knowledge abstracted from sensations. In other words, the "quiddity" of the thing perceived by sense is the proper object of the human intellect.[20]

This alone should suffice to assure us that we cannot form any proper representation of God. Since he is at the summit of actuality and immateriality, God can be but very imperfectly expressed by concepts abstracted from his creatures. They are material objects, their cause is not. The extreme difficulty of metaphysical knowledge has no other origin. To the extent that it deals with the divinity, it must strive to conceive immaterial objects, while the intellect of man cannot think without images abstracted from material things.

No wonder then that true metaphysicians are rare. Common sense does not rise above the level of imaginable realities, and, when it is a question of metaphysics, the *vulgus* includes many a mind eminent in other fields. Scientists, artists

of genius, great statesmen—all those who like to
proclaim: "I only know what I can see and touch,"
even though in other respects they may be eminent specimens of the human kind, are nevertheless unfit for metaphysical speculation.[21] Let us
add, for their consolation, that they are perfectly
normal men. Anyone who says, "I understand
nothing of what you call metaphysics," is quite
justified, and there is for him nothing to feel
ashamed of. But he should stop there. That one
does not see any light, may be a fact; to infer
from it that there is no light, is a *non sequitur*.

But this is not the whole problem. We often
speak of things of which, because they are immaterial, the essences escape us.[22] The case of God
is different because his whole essence is *to be*. In
trying to form some notion of God, we naturally
start from our knowledge of that which is most
perfect in his creatures. Now, the act of their acts
and the perfection of all their perfections is not
to be found in what they are, but in their very
existential actuality. Consequently, we must think
of God as of actual existence in its absolute perfection. This conclusion confronts us at the point
of confluence of philosophy and theology, of reason and revelation. The best we can say about
God is that *HE IS*. As God himself says in Exodus
3:14, his proper name is *QUI EST*.

But how can we conceive an *Is* that is neither

this nor that being, but only *is* and nothing else? With a slightly different meaning, but quite in the same vein, Augustine had already said of God: "He is not in this and that way, but he is, *IS*." [23] A rather puzzling statement indeed, for if you say "is," you can expect me to ask: is who? or, is what? Since the essence, or substance, of God is identically his pure act of being, such questions about him are bound to remain unanswered. And that cannot be helped. Since, in the case of God himself, the object of thought entirely transcends the mode of knowing proper to man, the most powerfully gifted metaphysical mind and the ordinary man find themselves in the same predicament. In its present condition the human mind is incapable of conceiving the *is* of anything apart from its concept of the thing that is.

Esse is intelligible in its own right; as the form of forms it is even more intelligible in itself than any other form; in fact, it is too intelligible for an intellect such as our own, which lacks the power of intellectual intuition required for the sight of purely intelligible objects. Hence the importance of the notion of "negative theology" in the doctrine of Saint Thomas. It is essential to Thomism and expressive of its very spirit.

A first way to misunderstand this aspect of the doctrine is to turn it into a complete agnosticism, as if, according to Thomas, we knew nothing at

all about God. It is not so. We have a positive
knowledge of God. First, arguing from his effects,
we know of him that he is. This already is very
important, but we even have positive information
about him. All that which is found in God's effects
necessarily is first in him as in their cause. So we
can be sure that every perfection found in creatures also is included in the creator. Only here
again we know *that* they are in him; *what* they
are in him, that is, *how* they are in him, we do not
know. We know only that God is what we call
intelligent, wise, good, powerful and all that
which it is better to be than not to be, but since
these perfections are in him identical with his
own *esse,* we cannot imagine under what form
such perfections are in him. To know that they
are in him, however, is positive knowledge. The
negative theology presupposes a positive theology; it needs such a theology, be it only so as to
be able to transcend it.

There is a more common way to misunderstand
the doctrine. Even among those who claim
Thomas Aquinas for their master, quite a few
hesitate to follow him completely along a way
which, as they see it, ends in a sort of agnosticism.
They willingly admit that, according to Thomas
Aquinas, we have but a very imperfect knowledge of the divine nature, but they nevertheless
maintain that we can form a positive notion of

what God is. I am not here attempting to provide the true answer to the problem; my only concern is with what Thomas himself has said on a point which, as I see it, is of decisive importance for a correct understanding of his doctrine, as well as, I beg to add, for the future of Christian theology itself. Now, what Thomas actually says is that the essence, quiddity, or whatness of God is something we do not know at all. He does not say that we do not know it much, or not well, or that we know it only a little; he says we simply do not know what it is *at all*.

The future of Christian theology has a stake in this problem because on this point of capital importance—how much do we know of God's nature?—Thomas follows the great theological tradition of the Greek Fathers of the Church, so that to deviate from it in our own days would be to raise, on the road to the desired reunion of the churches, an obstacle which in the authentic Thomism of Thomas himself, simply does not exist.

The source of the doctrine on this point is the passage of his *Mystica theologia,* in which Denis says that in this life our knowledge of God attains its point of perfection when by it we are united to him as unknown: *cum Deo quasi ignoto conjungimur*. And, Thomas adds, this happens when we know of God what he is not, while what

he is remains "utterly unknown." To signify that
ignorance in which our most sublime knowledge
of God consists, Scripture says of Moses that he
entered the obscurity wherein God is dwelling
(Exod. 20:21). Once more we are learning from
revelation the truth about God which reason investigates, and this time the truth at stake is that
in this life what it is for God to be remains to us
penitus ignotum.[24] The adverb *penitus* can mean
only one thing, namely, that we don't know at all.

On a still more general level, even the future
of religious thought has an interest in this question. To put it bluntly, the problem of philosophical atheism is at stake here. Some men complain
that they would like to think there is a God, but
that they cannot see him as we do. If that is their
only trouble, they can turn confidentally to the
theology of Thomas Aquinas. What he will teach
them is that so long as we still imagine what God
is, the object of our thought is not yet God. For
God is above all the beings we know or imagine.
He is even above being itself. To call God being
(*ens*), even the supreme being (*summum ens*),
is not to describe his essence, or that which he is,
but only to designate him as the cause of all
beings.

As a divine name, "being" signifies *esse* as proceeding from God into creatures,[25] and because
we know him only as their cause, we reach the

end of our theology when we say of him that he is "the very act of being," subsisting in the plenitude of its actuality.[26] That is what philosophy says, and no philosophy is safely protected against the dangers of anthropomorphism; but this also is what theology learns from Scripture. The true world of Thomism is a world whose very existence attests the presence of its cause; it is a world wide open to the free investigation of reason and by the same token it is to man a permanent reminder that its first cause is also his ultimate end.

Whatever question we may ask about the world of Saint Thomas, the answer must of necessity be: God. We began by wondering how it was that the same man could be equally certain of the truth of reason and the truth of faith. Our first approach to an answer was the remark that when it came to key questions about the world, man and his destiny, the teaching of Scripture confirmed and completed the conclusions slowly reached by rational inquiry by the greatest among the philosophers of the past. Revelation offers to us the knowledge—to be held as true by simple faith—of all that is necessary and sufficient to know in order to achieve salvation.

We then asked ourselves why that twofold kind of knowledge should be offered to man, and we seemed to find an answer in the very nature of man. Man is a living paradox. On the one hand, since he is created by God, man is finite; as such, he is naturally incapable of knowing the infinite being of God. On the other hand, man is an intellectual substance; as such he is capable of knowing all that which is, that is to say, the totality of being. Now—and this is the center of the whole doctrine—God himself has created that paradoxical disproportion between the only object able to appease man's desire, infinite being, and the finite powers of the human understanding.

The best explanation of the paradox is that when God created man in His own image—that is, as an intellectual substance—he foresaw the help His creature would need, and receive, to attain its end. So our second conclusion was that when the nature created by God is an intellect, the divine wisdom will not deny it the supernatural help without which the divine allpowerfulness would create it in vain. Hence the admirable harmony of revelation and reason, of nature and grace, since nature was created in view of grace which alone enables intellectual natures to attain their end.

And now, beyond those beings, we are reaching their cause. I say "beyond" for indeed the cause of being is above being. As we said, it is *esse*, the infinite *esse*, in which beings participate in a finite way. This is so true that it could almost do for a definition of being: *ens dicitur id quod finite participat esse;*[27] but of *esse* itself, precisely because it is beyond being, there is no definition. We know of it only that "to be" is the very essence of God.[28] The quiddity of God is his very act of being: *Quidditas Dei est suum ipsum esse.*[29] To understand this supreme truth is to know that we do not know what God is; and to know that, is also to reach the summit of human knowledge in this life: *et hoc est ultimum et perfectissimum nostrae cognitionis in hac vita.*[30]

Such is the last word of Thomism, a truly sacred doctrine indeed, which Thomas himself summed up with his usual lucidity. There is a threefold knowledge of the divinity: The first is science and philosophy through which, by the natural light of reason, man ascends to a knowledge of God through creatures. The second is faith in the divine truth that descends upon us by mode of revelation, that is, not as a truth to be seen, but as words to be believed. The third knowledge of God is eternal life, during which the human mind is elevated to the perfect sight of the things revealed.[31]

Just now, however, we are not perpetually passing from the first mode of knowledge to the second one, but are walking in the light of both, and since "the way of ascent and descent is the same" we are at each moment at some point common to both. But intellectual knowledge is our own knowledge; the very same intellect is ascending to a knowledge of God from creatures and struggling toward a still higher one through its understanding of the revealed truth; so, in Thomas' own words, "we must proceed in the same way in the things above reason which are believed, as we proceeded with the investigation of God by reason." [32] For indeed faith is there to lead reason to perfect knowledge. In eternal life, understanding, not faith, will have the last word.

CHAPTER IV

A Living Thomism

Is there a future in sight for Thomism, and, if there is one, what kind of future could it be?

There are many obstacles on Thomism's road to success. The first is its religious inspiration. The difficulty is so obvious that ever since the fourteenth century many Thomists have attempted to separate the philosophical from the religious in the doctrine of Thomas Aquinas. They hoped to provide a Thomistic philosophy completely distinct from Thomistic theology.

Their intention was good; but if what I have said in the preceding lectures is true, the attempt was doomed to failure. True enough, Thomas has introduced a clear-cut distinction between reason and faith, philosophy and theology. But far from inferring from this distinction that they should be kept apart, Thomas always thought that the best thing for them to do was to live in a sort of symbiosis in which each profited from its association with the other. I know that many philosophers refuse to have anything to do with religion, but that does not prove that they are right, even as philosophers. At any rate, I also know that, judged from the point of view of the spirit of Thomism, they are certainly wrong.

What should we do then to make Thomism acceptable to such men? The answer is simple: we should teach it as it is. There is for us no other choice, at least if it is Thomism that we want to teach. Of course we cannot cause men to believe in the truth of revelation, but Thomas does not think we should worry about that. However intimately associated with faith it may be in our own mind, our philosophy, as philosophy, stands on its own merits. Perfected in us by faith, natural reason can help others to perceive the reasonableness of faith, and that is what Thomas Aquinas was hoping his theology would achieve: "For though it is not in our power to know by ourselves the things of faith, nevertheless, if we do what we can, that is to say, if we follow the guidance of natural reason (*ut scilicet ductum naturalis rationis sequamus*), God will not fail to give us what is necessary to us (*Deus non deficiet a nobis quod nobis necessarium est*).[1] When I find myself wondering what I should do about the situation, my personal answer is: "Do what Thomas himself says: follow the lead of natural reason as far as it takes you; God will do the rest."

A more formidable obstacle is a purely philosophical one. Even apart from the association of Thomism with theology, many philosophers are likely to find it the wrong sort of philosophy because it is realistic, whereas today only the idealistic can hope to be accepted.

This is the more true because idealism enjoys the privilege of constructing systems, for it is easier to systematize notions than things. Systems always attract attention, and, because they can be learned and taught, they stand a good chance of surviving in the memory of the generations to come.[2] If I say, "Descartes," you will answer: "*I think,* therefore I am." Likewise, Leibnitz means monadology, Malebranche spells occasionalism, Spinoza, substance, Spencer, evolution, and so on. Systems are interesting to read and easy to teach, but has any philosophical system ever been true? Toward the end of the nineteenth century, a German philosopher by the name of Franz Brentano began to wonder how long the chain of the mutually destructive systems of philosophy was going to continue. Kant had just been replaced by Fichte, Fichte by Schelling, Schelling by Hegel, and Hegel by Schopenhauer. Hoping to bring the philosophical merry-go-round to a stop, Brentano suggested as a remedy a general return to the realism of the Greeks.[3] This meant that for us as already for Aristotle, the method of philosophy should be the same as that of the science of nature, to wit, a rational interpretation of observed facts. The result of Brentano's experiment is conclusive: himself a good psychologist, Brentano left no system to which his name could be attached, so that today he is practically forgotten.

I must confess that I know of no remedy to the difficulty. If philosophical realism is right, we cannot turn Thomism into a wrong philosophy in order to increase the number of its supporters. Philosophy simply is not the kind of conceptual poetry they call a philosophical "system." Philosophy is wisdom, and wisdom is not poetry. Neither is it positive science, nor ethics, nor economics, nor politics. A true philosopher may well be neither a scientist nor a successful industrialist, nor a celebrated statesman. When asked to say what he knows, the true philosopher modestly answers with Socrates: nothing. And indeed his own function is not to know any particular kind of things; rather, it is to start from the cognitions gained by other men in the various and changing fields of knowledge and action; it is to clarify these cognitions, to criticize them and to order them by relating them to first causes. Like science, philosophy is about things, not cognitions, yet what is left of science, unless it thus unifies itself in the light of philosophical reflection, is but a heap of uncritical and disjointed pieces of information.

Thomas Aquinas was well aware of this truth and that is the reason his personal contributions to philosophy belong chiefly in the field of metaphysics, which is the science of the first principles of reality as well as of knowledge. He never pretended he was introducing into philosophy a new first principle. The project would have seemed preposterous to him. For him it was one and the same thing to think, to think of some thing, and to think of it as of a being. Because being attends all our representations, every true philosophy must be a philosophy of being.

Thomas also knew that reflection on being necessarily leads to the notion of the act in virtue of which being is, and is being, namely that of *esse*. This conclusion leads to no system, but it throws light on the manifold of reality and permits us to order it. If we want to rejuvenate Thomism, the first thing for us to do is to revive its interpretation of the first principle; if we do, our experience will probably be that we ourselves stand more in need of being rejuvenated by Thomism than it does by us.

The second mark of a living Thomism immediately follows from the first one because in beings *to be* comes first, and to be is an act; the real world outside us is not made up of static essences but of acting, operating and causing beings. In Thomas' own words, "from the very fact that something actually is, it is active": *ex hoc ipso quod aliquid in actu est, activum est.*

Without essences, finite beings would not be possible; and it is true that, as the Schoolmen used to say, the essences are operating and living things, but they act and operate only because they are, and they are only because each and every one of them is actuated by its own act of being. It would be silly to attribute to Thomas Aquinas the great intuitions of today's science. He was no scientist, but at the level of philosophical insight he certainly entertained a general view of the world of nature attuned to that of modern physics. To him the last word about physical reality was not extension in space, nor was it matter, nor pattern and shape, but rather it was act, *energeia,* or as we say today, energy. He only would add to the scientific view of the world a purely metaphysical one, to wit, that the act of all acts and the energy of all energies is *"to be."* And indeed, if they *were not,* things could neither act nor operate; there simply would be nothing.

If we succeed in seeing things in the light of

that capital notion, the whole order of action assumes a new importance and even a new meaning. We are naturally inclined to see the world as consisting of things to each of which a certain number of operations can be attributed. In such a view, the thing is the core of reality. Not so in the universe of Thomas Aquinas, wherein all substance is in view of its operation: *omnis substantia est propter suam operationem.* In other words, the thing is not there in view of itself but rather in view of its acts. Common sense here agrees with metaphysical intuition. Why do we say "handsome is that handsome does," if not because, for man, to do is fully to be? Only in his acting does every one of us fully actualize his being. Now that is the authentic teaching of Thomas Aquinas: the ultimate perfection of the thing is its operation; *operatio enim est ultima perfectio rei.*[4]

One of the main perils that threaten Thomism is the tendency of too many Thomists to mistake the world for a collection of substances inertly subsisting in a kind of glorious inactivity. Hence the rise of the modern philosophies of "action" that are intended to stress a notion their authors consider badly neglected by Thomas Aquinas. If they think that Thomism does not recognize the importance of action in beings, I wonder what Thomas could have done to make it more clear.

He has expressed it in a sentence which, for even such a master of philosophical style, is uncommonly packed with substance. I am afraid it defies translation, but here it is: "Just as the act of being (*ipsum esse*) is a certain actuality of the essence, so also operating is an actuality of the power or energy to operate. For such indeed is the reason both are in act, namely, the essence inasmuch as it is, and the power because it operates."[5] It is therefore in their operations that finite beings attain the whole actuality of which they are capable, and no wonder, since to be is for them the act of all the acts.

A last objection to Thomism, or rather against its chances of survival, is still more serious than the preceding ones. It is the actual failure of most of us to provide proofs of its continuing vitality. And indeed, a great deal has been done to keep it alive in schools, to defend it against adverse criticism and, more often still, to prove that Thomism is right by demonstrating that the rest is wrong. The best thing we are doing along those lines probably is the present effort of many of us to clear up the meaning of the first principles which are at one and the same time those of Thomism, of the mind and of reality.

This is a praiseworthy undertaking, for indeed the understanding of a philosophy hangs on that of its principles, but the cognition of the first principles is not the whole of philosophical knowledge. True enough, it is its higher part, but even the highest part of a whole is not the whole. Complete philosophical wisdom is the knowledge of reality seen in the light of first principles and as related to its first cause. If what I have just said is true, the principles themselves as contained in our knowledge attain the fullness of their being only when they are actualizing themselves in their operation. To know is to know something. To understand a principle is to understand through that principle. I know being only in the acts whereby I am knowing beings.

To reduce Thomism to the contemplation of its principles would deprive it of all actual content. A chance remark of Thomas Aquinas on the object of the beatific vision can be quoted in confirmation of this truth. "The ultimate felicity of man," Thomas says, "cannot consist in the contemplation which depends on the understanding of the principles, for that is a most imperfect contemplation, being most universal and limited to the knowledge of things in potency. Besides, that is only the beginning of human inquiry, not its end, since we owe it to nature, not to our own effort to discover truth." [6]

Translated into plain language, the objection means that ever since the end of the sixteenth century, scholasticism has tended to become a more or less repetitious kind of school teaching, perfect in its form and in that respect often superior to most of the more modern philosophies, but poverty-stricken in its contents, unable to produce new ideas and to play its part in the rational interpretation of the modern world. To put it bluntly, the main objection to modern scholasticism is its sterility.

On this point, I think we should plead partially guilty. Born in schools, created by schoolmen for classroom consumption, scholasticism soon conceived of itself as identical with philosophy itself. Now the end of philosophical studies is not for us to have learned philosophy. Just as physics is not about physics, but about nature, so also philosophy is not about philosophy but about reality understood in the light of philosophical principles. To philosophize is actually to apply these principles to a rational interpretation of reality. Because it is too much of a teaching and not enough of a training, slowly but surely scholasticism is dying of anemia.

When we realize the danger of the situation, we are inclined to blame it on the principles of the doctrine. Then we try to modernize them, but the result is disastrous, for indeed the principles of scholasticism are perfectly sound; we are to blame for neglecting to put them to good use. The modern Thomist too often is like unto a man holding a lamp, lost in the contemplation of its light and complaining that he sees nothing. Let us only turn our light on the world of things around us, and we shall have plenty to see and to say.

That is what Thomas Aquinas himself so successfully did in his own time. Having inherited from Aristotle a sound philosophy, he wisely decided to apply its principles, not to the ancient world of the Philosopher, but to the modern world in which he himself happened to live. Those two worlds were separated by a decisive event, namely, the Christian revelation. In this revelation, philosophy was confronted with something of which Aristotle had no idea. In order to understand this event, philosophy had to share in the task of *sacra doctrina,* which consisted in opening the minds of unbelievers to the saving truth, as far as could be done by expressing it in the language of natural reason. Hence the notorious formula: philosophy is the handmaid of theology.

To the extent that he used similar expressions— for I do not think this one is literally to be found in Saint Thomas himself—he never intended them as a definition of philosophy. To him philosophy essentially was that of Aristotle, who had no Christian theology to serve, but even in Aristotle philosophy was tending toward a theology of its own, and that is the reason Thomas always conceives the relationship between theology and the philosophical sciences as analogous to that obtaining, within philosophy itself, between those sciences and metaphysics.

Wisdom sent her maids to invite guests to the tower (Prov. 9:3).[7] Taken in itself this is not a description of the task of philosophy, but for an intelligent handmaid there is no better opportunity to learn than to serve an intelligent mistress. Had he contented himself with teaching the philosophy of Aristotle, Thomas Aquinas could not have done better than faithfully to repeat the doctrine of the master. He would now be to us one more of those many peripatetics whose names dot the history of late scholasticism. On the contrary, Thomas Aquinas set out to bring the teaching of Aristotelianism to a more complete realization of its truth, because the object of his own philosophical reflections was not a philosophy but a religion.

This creative activity of Thomism is what we now need to revive, and the only way to revive it is to put its principles to good use again; but this time—and I am speaking as a philosopher rather than as a theologian—we need to turn our attention to the object of philosophical speculation. That object is nature, and although in itself nature has probably changed but little since the thirteenth century, our knowledge of it is very different from what it was in the mind of Thomas Aquinas. Our mental universe, as William James would call it, has long ceased to be the same. We now know many things Thomas Aquinas never heard of.

First of all, we now know that Aristotle had but an incomplete knowledge of what it is scientifically to know. Himself an excellent observer, he was no mathematician; he was fond of classifying, but much less fond of measuring. In mathematics, astronomy, cosmology, biology and anthropology, a twelve-year-old child of today is full of information completely unknown to Thomas Aquinas.

Furthermore, six centuries of modern history have considerably modified our perspective on the nature of political, social and economical life. Changes have not always been for the better. In its efforts toward more knowledge and a better way of life, mankind normally proceeds by trial and error. Everything man does is purposeful, but he may be misguided in his purposes and still more often in his choice of the means. Enormous material has thus been accumulating since the time of Thomas Aquinas, and a living Thomism should devote itself to the urgent task of criticizing it, interpreting it and ordering it in the light of permanently valid principles, that is to say, of the Thomistic metaphysics of being.

Even as a handmaid of theology (Thomas once

called his thought its "vassal") a living Thomism could render signal services, if only in dissuading theology from wasting its time interpreting a physical universe that has long ceased to exist. Natural theology is fraught with concepts and images inherited from popular beliefs and from now outdated scientific views of the world. By ridding the imagination of those transitory mythologies, a well informed Thomism could help *sacra doctrina* to achieve a higher degree of theological purity. There is no point in continuing to state the *prima via* of Thomas Aquinas as though the sun were revolving around the earth or as though the principle of inertia had never been discovered.

But these would be complicated examples to discuss, so let us content ourselves with simpler ones. Does the word "heaven" mean to us what it meant to a thirteenth century theologian? He knew it was "above." But, today, where is above? And by the by, where is hell? Such scientifically minded theologians as William of Auvergne and Saint Albert the Great were already busy demythicizing some currently accepted popular notions, but they could do so only in the light of thirteenth century science. For instance, speaking of hell, Albert still thought it was "below," not far from the center of the earth and somewhat to the left. But today where is "below"? Were he still with us, Albert would have to admit that the adverb no longer makes sense in that application.

A still simpler question is: where is the earthly paradise? Apart from the cautious Origen, who understood it in a spiritual sense, most of the theologians thought it was *somewhere,* but where it was, they did not know. After pushing it east toward India, then south toward Ethiopia, they felt rather puzzled when a better knowledge of the explored parts of the earth failed to ascertain its location. Thomas Aquinas was well aware of the problem, but he also was very cautious about such questions. Before following Origen's allegorical interpretation of Scripture, Thomas wanted to be absolutely sure that the earthly paradise was nowhere to be found on the surface of the earth. He said that the fact that it had not yet been discovered was no proof that it did not exist. It might have escaped detection because access to it was difficult. That place—*locus ille,* Thomas called it—was secluded from our lands by impassable seas, desert wastes, mountains, or stormy and uninhabitable regions. Such might well be the reason, Thomas added, why no writers had ever mentioned its location despite careful explorations of the habitable parts of the earth.[8]

Today, Amazonia looks like our last chance to find the lost paradise. But the chance is slim. This simple case can help us realize, when more important questions arise, how positive information can purify the very substance of religious belief from the incidental imagery which often goes along with it.

What is true of theology is still more obviously true of metaphysical knowledge. Modern physics has deeply transformed traditional notions of matter, mass, energy, and the like. Microphysics is now suffering from a certain disorder because of the speed of its progress, but it has changed our view of the world perhaps still more radically than astronomy ever did. There never was a time when the reflections of scientists themselves on the nature of physical causality provided as much food for philosophical thought as the controversies among leaders of scientific inquiry in our own day. The names of Max Planck, Heisenberg, Niels Bohr, Einstein, Fermi, de Broglie and many others suffice to evoke the memory of those scientific discussions. Positive science itself has become a highly specialized business. Neither the theologian nor even the philosopher can be expected to master the scientific techniques at play in these controversies. To do so is none of their business.

On the other hand, the business of the scientist is not to provide a clear philosophical elucidation of the principles involved in his own scientific theories. Only the philosopher is qualified to do so. A remarkable example of that kind of work was provided, twenty years ago or so, by a chemist who was neither a theologian nor a metaphysician, but a mind remarkably gifted for philosophical speculation. I am thinking of Emile Meyerson and of his great book, *Identity and Reality*.[9]

In the fields of the philosophy of nature, of political economy and of the so-called "human sciences," the example of Jacques Maritain clearly shows how it is still possible today to renovate ancient concepts and to open new fields of investigation.[10] The philosophy of art, illustrated by the same philosopher, clearly shows that in certain cases Thomism is bound to create if it is still to live. For indeed Thomas himself has said precious little, if anything, about the fine arts. In all these fields, modern Thomists are confronted with problems unknown to their master and for which no answers can be found readymade in his writings.

In the thirteenth century, a great adversary of the theologians Albert the Great and Thomas Aquinas called them the two philosophical leaders of the time: *praecipui viri in philosophia.* The trouble with Christian philosophers of today is that those of us who know theology seldom know science, while among those who know science very few know theology. Many of the latter think they do, but that is not the same thing,

not even when these self-appointed theologians
happen to be priests.

And yet I believe there is hope. A striking in-
novation took place in the history of the Church
when the huge task of bringing Christian philosophy up to date was assumed by the popes. After
the somewhat unpopular *Syllabus* of Pope Pius
IX, an almost uninterrupted chain of encyclical
letters has reminded the world that the teaching
function in the Church belongs properly to the
bishops and that the Pope is the Bishop of Rome.
The names of Leo XIII, Pius XI, Pius XII and
John XXIII call to mind many epoch-making encyclicals, entirely different in style from the ancient ones, in which the leading moral and social
problems of our own times are handled with wisdom, authority and a doctrinal audacity which
perhaps comes more easily to a pope than to any
lesser teacher in the Church.[11]

It did not take long for Paul VI to make it
known that the recently established tradition
would be continued. And no wonder, since the
first of those epoch-making documents was the
celebrated encyclical *Aeterni Patris*, in which
Pope Leo XIII, nearly one hundred years ago,
proclaimed Thomas Aquinas the patron saint of
Catholic schools, and soon after, the Common
Doctor of the Church. Then the popes waited for
us to do the work, but when they saw that not

much of it was being done, they decided to do it themselves. Still, like Wisdom, they too are inviting all of us to the tower. The truths which the successors of Saint Peter will sanction tomorrow by their authority need to be prepared by the personal efforts of countless obscure philosophers and theologians of today, and this is our own responsibility.

The popes have repeatedly called upon us to share in that great collective task to be performed by all Christians under their leadership and their authority. If the call is heard, there will be a living Thomism; we are all invited to answer the call in the fullness of our goodwill and to the full measure of our limited capacities. If we do, the success does not matter; it will be what God wants it to be. Provided only that we remember that we are His right-hand men, He will do the rest.

Notes

Chapter I

[1] M.-M. d'Hendecourt, "Laberthonnière," *Revue de Métaphysique et de Morale*, 63 (1961), p. 53. I have recalled elsewhere what Laberthonnière (who was an admirable priest) once told me after attending a lecture of mine on scholasticism in which Thomas occupied a prominent place: "Je le hais, c'est un malfaiteur." But we have a more significant token of his enmity toward philosophy—any philosophy—which pretends to posit itself apart from religion:

A great admirer and friend of Lucien Laberthonnière was Maurice Blondel, whose thesis of 1893, *L'Action*, was welcomed by Laberthonnière with unbounded admiration and unrestricted approval. As years went by, Blondel felt the need to revise that first expression of his thought. In the meantime he had become better acquainted with scholasticism, especially Thomism, of which at first he had been severely critical without knowing Thomism any too well. Hence the later works of Blondel wherein he strives to effect a conciliation between the traditional positions of scholasticism and the earlier formulations of his own thought.

The result was fatal, if not to a friendship which nothing could really destroy, at least to the atmosphere of intimate unity of soul and mind that had so long obtained between Blondel and Laberthonnière. See the letter of Blondel to Laberthonnière, May 29, 1927, in *Maurice Blondel–Lucien Laberthonnière, Correspondence philosophique*, ed. by Claude Tresmontant (Paris: Editions du Seuil, 1961), p. 352. In the letter of November 9, 1927, Blondel has perfectly analyzed the ultimate implications of their doctrinal disagreement. The question at stake finally was: Can there be a philosophy really distinct from religion if the distinction between nature and grace "is at bottom without justification" (*"n'a aucune raison profonde d'être"*)? (*op. cit.*, p. 354). Cf. p. 355, the moving passage in which Blondel tells

103

Laberthonnière what he wishes his old friend would say. But Laberthonnière never said it.

[2] On Eusebius of Cesarea, see my *History of Christian Philosophy in the Middle Ages* (New York: Random House, 1955), p. 579. On Justin, *op. cit.*, pp. 11–14 and p. 555, note 10. Cf. the often misunderstood "Christian Gnosticism" of Clement of Alexandria, *op. cit.*, pp. 31–33; on the theme that philosophy was to the Greeks what the divine Law was to the Jews, *op. cit.*, p. 567, notes 7 and 8, references.

[3] Thomas Aquinas, *In I Sent.*, Prol., q. 1, a. 1. N.B.: in all the following notes, the name will be omitted when the reference is to Aquinas.

[4] *Loc. cit.*, solutio.

[5] *De veritate catholicae fidei contra gentiles* (to be quoted as *Contra gentiles*), I, 4, 3. Book, chapter and paragraph are numbered as in the English translation of the work edited under the direction of A. C. Pegis (4 books in 5 vols.; New York: Doubleday & Co., Image Books, 1955–57).

[6] *In decem libros Aristotelis ad Nicomachum*, X, 9, ed. R. M. Spiazzi, O.P., 2133–36.

[7] Even in our own irreligious and unmetaphysical times, great minds sometimes wonder at the twofold fact that there is intellectual knowledge and that the world of nature is intelligible to the mind. What is eternally incomprehensible about the world, Einstein says, is its comprehensibility: "Man kan sagen: das ewig Unbegreifliche an der Welt ist ihre Begreiflichkeit" (A. Einstein, *Zeitschrift für freie deutsche Forschung* [Paris, 1938], I, pp. 6–7). The text is quoted, with comments, in L. Lévy-Bruhl, *Les carnets de notes de Lucien Lévy-Bruhl* (Paris: Presses Universitaires, 1949), pp. 70–72. The title of Einstein's article was, *"Physik und Realität."* In L. Lévy-Bruhl's own words, the import of the great physicist's position is that "the intelligibility of the world is itself unintelligible." Thomas Aquinas simply refuses to consider that unintelligibility as final; but the possibility of intelligibility in physics is accountable in terms of metaphysics and theology only.

[8] *In Job*, 13, lect. 2; ed. Fretté, vol. XVIII, p. 90. The text commented upon is Job 13:3 and 13:13–22.

⁹ *In I Sent.*, Prol., q. 1, a. 3, quaestiuncula 3, solutio.

¹⁰ *Summa theologiae*, II-II, 1, 1, resp. One of the reasons for the endless controversies on the nature of theology as a science in Thomism, is the accidental fact that the first question of the *Summa theologiae* presupposes the knowledge of what will be said in the IIa-IIae, where the object and nature of faith are explicitly dealt with. This theology of faith has been included in the *Basic Writings of Saint Thomas Aquinas*, translated and annotated by A. C. Pegis (New York: Random House, 1945). Anyone who really wants to understand the doctrine should apply himself to the personal study of those questions. The passage under discussion states exactly: "What properly and directly belongs to the object of faith is that through which man obtains beatitude" (Pegis, *op. cit.*, II, p. 1084). Cf. "those things are in themselves of faith, which order us directly to eternal life" (*Summa theologiae*, II-II, 1, 6, ad 1m; *op. cit.*, II, p. 1064). This is the basis of the whole theology of Thomas Aquinas.

¹¹ ". . . theologia, id est scientia divina, quia praecipuum in ea cognitorum est Deus, quae alto nomine dicitur metaphysica." *In Boethii de Trinitate*, II, 1, 1, resp.

¹² *Summa theologiae*, I, 1, 1, ad 2m. The exactly opposite notion is found in Descartes, who considered scholastic medicine and scholastic theology as *"scientias annexas"* to scholastic philosophy (*Oeuvres complètes*, ed. Adam-Tannery, vol. VIII,² p. 34).

¹³ *Summa theologiae*, II-II, 4, 1, resp.

¹⁴ *Summa theologiae*, II-II, 2, 5, *sed contra*. Cf. a. 3, *sed contra*. On faith as a human answer to a divine invitation, II-II, 2, 9, ad 3m: "Ille qui credit habet sufficiens inductivum ad credendum; inducitur enim auctoritate divinae doctrinae miraculis confirmatae, et *quod plus est, interiori instinctu Dei invitantis.*"

¹⁵ Even in philosophical matters, a sermon could be preached on the small number of the elect. On this point, Thomas closely follows the Jewish Rabbi Moses Maimonides and his *Guide for the Perplexed*, I, 34 (*History of Christian Philosophy in the Middle Ages*, p. 650, note 38). The doctrine reappears in *Contra gen-*

tiles, I, 4, 3, but also in other words of Thomas Aquinas, for instance, in *In III Sent.,* d. 24, q. 1, a. 3, quaestiuncula 3, solutio, and in abbreviated form, in *Summa theologiae,* I, 1, 1: "Even as regards those truths about God which human reason can investigate, it was necessary (*necessarium fuit*) that man be taught by a divine revelation. For the truth about God, such as reason can know it, would only be known by a few, and that after a long time, and with the admixture of many errors; whereas man's whole salvation, which is in God, depends upon the knowledge of this truth" (Pegis, *Basic Writings,* I, p. 6).

[16] The whole doctrine was summed up by Thomas Aquinas from the beginning of his career, in *In III Sent.,* d. 24, q. 1, a. 3, quaestiuncula 3, solutio 1. In faith, there are certain things that are above human reason absolutely (*simpliciter*), and faith essentially is one of those things (*de quibus essentialiter est fides*); then there are other things that are above the reason of this and that man, though not above the reason of every man, and in both cases it was necessary that faith be given (*et ad utraque necessarium fuit dari fidem*). In support of this position, Thomas gives two reasons that are the very roots of his own theology: (1) a supernatural knowledge is required if the end to be reached is supernatural; (2) in view of that supernatural knowledge given to man by the grace of faith, a natural knowledge to be perfected by that grace had to be given.

In this all-embracing view of the general economy of salvation, Thomas sees the relationship of the natural knowledge of God to revelation as analogous to that of human nature to grace. Carefully observe the wording of the statement: "Just as, in perfecting our affections, grace presupposes a nature to be perfected, so also a natural knowledge is laid down under faith" (*ita et fidei substernitur naturalis cognitio*). Faith presupposes that knowledge (Thomas says: a "natural" knowledge, not necessarily a "philosophical" one) and reason can furnish proofs (this time, by philosophy) such as: God exists, God is one, incorporeal, intelligent, and such other things. If one cannot know those things by reasoning, faith will sufficiently incline him to assent to them by faith.

"To sum up, there is a natural knowledge of God which, in some men, can be turned into a demonstrated philosophical knowledge, but to the extent that such knowledge is necessarily required for salvation, God has revealed it to all men. So they all can assent to it, and faith inclines their reason to do so; this assent of reason is, as elicited by faith, a rational assent, but a non-philosophical one" (*et ad hoc fides sufficienter inclinat, ut qui rationem ad hoc habere non potest, fide eis assentiat*). Thomas presently adds: "And this was necessary for five reasons, as Rabbi Moses says, I, 33," etc. Cf. *Quaestiones disputatae de veritate*, q. 14, a. 9, ad 8m.

[17] The fact that interreactions take place within the mind between reason and faith has always been known. The doctrines of Augustine and Anselm rest upon that fact. The text of Peter Lombard, commented upon by Thomas Aquinas as well as by all the other masters of theology, expressly mentions it in Book III, d. 24. Among the things held by faith, some are understood by the natural reason, some are not: "Quaedam ergo fide creduntur, quae intelliguntur naturali ratione, quaedam vero, quae non intelliguntur." As quoted from *In III Sent.*, d. 24 in Fr. Pelster, S. J., S. *Thomas de Aquino Quaestiones de natura fidei* (Opuscula et textus) (Monasterii, 1926), p. 16.

"Unde colligitur: non possent sciri et intelligi credenda quaedam, nisi prius credantur, et quaedam non credi nisi prius intelligantur, et ipsa per fidem amplius intelligi" (*op. cit.*, p. 17) ("certain things could not be believed and understood, unless they first were believed, but there are some other things that cannot be believed unless they first are understood, and themselves are further understood by faith"). How this works in concrete reality is a matter of cases to be discussed by the psychologist. Thomas was chiefly concerned with the general, which alone is an object of scientific knowledge, but he was aware of the existence of that class of problems; he even touches on some of them occasionally: *Quaestiones disputatae*, q. 14, a. 9, ad 9m. Cf. *Summa theologiae*, II-II, 1, 4, ad 3m.

[18] "Cum ergo in viribus animae voluntas habeat locum primi motoris, actus ejus est prior quodammodo actibus aliorum virium" (*In I Sent.*, d. 23, q. 3, quaestiuncula 3,

solutio). This fully justifies the opinion of Fr. Ceslas Pera, O. P., that charity is the central force of Thomistic dynamism: "la carità come forza centrale del dinamismo tomista." Contemplation is the goal, but love is the active force that drives us to it.

[19] "Ex imperio voluntatis intellectus credibilibus assentit" (*Summa theologiae*, II-II, 4, 2, ad 1m). Cf. "credere est actus intellectus secundum quod movatur a voluntate ad assentiendum" (*loc. cit.*, resp).

[20] *Summa theologiae*, II-II, 4, 3, resp.

[21] *Loc. cit.*, ad 1m: "Caritas dicitur esse forma fidei, inquantum informet actum ipsius." This abstract formula means that the act of faith, when it is as it should be, is thoroughly impregnated with love. Charity prompts it, directs it toward its end, causes it to adhere to its object, and inspires it with a desire more and more intimately to penetrate its very substance. On this essential aspect of the doctrine I know of no better introduction than the pages devoted to it by Fr. M.-D-Chenu, O. P., in *Saint Thomas d'Aquin et la théologie*, pp. 54–57, 65–71. I only beg to suggest that these pages written with a perceptible anxiety to convey to the reader the vital importance of the truth at stake, should be read with extreme attention and, on account of their doctrinal density, meditated upon till their content is thoroughly assimilated. Of course, the doctrine is theological in its very substance, and because charity informs natural reason through faith, any discussion on the controverted notion of "Christian philosophy" that does not take the theological point of view into account, is bound to be irrelevant.

[22] "Fides, quantum in se est, ad omnia quae fidem concomitantur, vel sequuntur, vel praecedunt, sufficienter inclinat." *In III Sent.*, d. 24, q. 1, a. 2, quaestiuncula 3, solutio 2.

[23] "Alio modo, ratio humana potest se habere ad voluntatem credentis consequenter. Cum enim homo habet promptam voluntatem ad credendum, diligit veritatem creditam, et super ea excogitat, et amplectitur, si quas rationes ad hoc invenire potest. Et, quantum ad hoc, ratio humana non excludit meritum fidei, sed est signum

majoris meriti" (*Summa theologiae*, II-II, 2, 10, resp).
Cf.: If a man who has a demonstration of the existence
of God remains willing to believe it on the sole authority
of God, his merit is not diminished (*loc. cit.*, ad 1m).
Even though the demonstrations diminished the merit of
faith, they would leave the merit of charity intact, since,
by charity, the will remains ready to believe the truth
if it were not seen (*loc. cit.*, ad 2m).

²⁴ See the whole passage, *In Boet. de Trinit.*, pro-
oemium, 2, 2, resp. The distinction of the disciplines is
clear: "sicut sacra doctrina fundatur super lumen fidei,
ita philosophia super lumen naturale rationis" (*op. cit.*,
prooem., 2, 3, resp.); but since philosophy is quasi-
totally ordained to the cognition of God, its highest object is the same as that of sacred doctrine, and this makes
it unwise for philosophy not to avail itself of what sacred
doctrine has learned from God himself concerning God.

The distinction of those two disciplines is less that of
two different sciences (since they are about the same
object) than between a science (philosophy) and wisdom (sacred doctrine). Now wisdom is not distinguished
from science as from a contrary, but as something that
is added to it (*op. cit.*, prooem., 2, 2, ad 1m). The unbeliever is free to neglect the teaching of a revelation in
which he does not believe; the Thomist, who professes
the Christian faith, cannot keep his science of God separate from the wisdom that "orders and regulates all the
other sciences" (*ibid.*).

Sacred doctrine possesses all the characteristics of
a science, but it is also a wisdom and, as such, is distinct
from mere science. In fact, it is the "*scientia sanctorum*"
(Wisd. 10:10), that is to say, the "*scientia fidei*," because
the science of the saints can be no other than the science
of that by which the sanctified (*sancti*) are distinguished from the impious (*impii*), which is faith: *In
Boet. de Trinit.*, prooem., 2, 2, sed contra 2.

Chapter II

¹ "Ipsaque prima philosophia tota ordinatur ad Dei
cognitionem sicut ad ultimum finem" (*Contra gentiles*,

III, 25, 9). The next quotation is taken from *Summa theologiae*, I, 16, 6, ad 1m: "nihil subsistens est majus mente rationali, nisi Deus."

[2] *Summa theologiae*, I, 93, 2, 6, 8 and 9. The technical justification is as follows: Beings are defined by the genus and the difference. The ultimate difference is what assigns to them their species within the genus. Now, in the case of man the specific difference is rationality and intellectuality. Consequently, only the intellectual creatures are made in the image of God. The argument is summarized by Cajetan in his commentary on I, 93, 3: "Solae creaturae intellectuales assimilantur Deo, ut intelligit et sapit; ergo solae creaturae intellectuales assimilantur Deo secundum quasi ultimam differentiam; ergo solae assimilantur secundum speciem. Ergo solae sunt ad imaginem."

Let us add two remarks: First, resemblance by mode of image is between man and God, not conversely. It is a resemblance between that which defines the species man, taken in its ultimate determination (intellectuality), and the very science and wisdom of God. Secondly, the biblical notion of the *image* of God in man is foreign to the doctrine of Aristotle, and it is the central notion around which the Thomistic notion of the created world entirely revolves. Epistemology and noetics are tied up with it: *Signatum est super nos lumen vultus tui, Domine* (Ps. 4:7). It accounts for the possibility of man's supernatural destiny. It is the reason the vision of God is naturally desired by all intellectual substances, man as well as angels. In fine, it is the reason that supernatural destiny is *possible* for such creatures, because, being created in God's image, their ultimate felicity consists in the same operation as the felicity of God, namely, intellectual contemplation.

Here is the whole doctrine in a nutshell: "et ideo intellectualis natura attingit ad imitationem divinam, in qua quodammodo consistit species naturae ejus, et inde est quod in eadem operatione ponimus ultimam felicitatem intellectualis creaturae, in qua est felicitas Dei, scilicet in contemplatione intellectiva; et ideo sola intellectualis natura rationabiliter ad imaginem Dei dicitur esse" (*In II Sent.*, d. 16, q. 1, a. 2, resp.). On the

Augustinian roots of the doctrine, see Anton C. Pegis, *At the Origins of the Thomistic Notion of Man* (The Saint Augustine Lecture, 1962; New York: Macmillan, 1963).

[3] Thomas has explained this point with perfect clearness in a passage that sums up his whole view of the final cause of creation: "The human intellect, to which it is connatural to derive its knowledge from sensible things, is not able through itself to reach the vision of the divine substance in itself, which is above all sensible things and, indeed, improportionately above all other things. Yet, because man's perfect good is that he somehow know God, lest such a noble creature might seem to be created to no purpose, as being unable to reach its own end, there is given to man a certain way through which he can rise to the knowledge of God: so that, since the perfections of God descend in a certain order from the highest summit of things—God—man may progress in the knowledge of God by beginning with lower things and gradually ascending. Now, even in bodily movements the way of descending is the same as the way of ascending, distinguished by beginning and end." *Contra gentiles*, IV, 1, 1; translated by Ch. J. O'Neil, in *On the Truth of the Catholic Faith* (New York: Image Books, 1956), V, p. 35.

We now know why philosophy spontaneously ordains itself to the cognition of God: the end of man is the vision of God and he finds himself in a universe so ordered that to progress in its knowledge is to progress in the knowledge of God.

[4] Thomas is almost overgenerous in granting to Plato and Aristotle the knowledge of some of the attributes of the Christian God. The philosophers did not, properly speaking, *believe* that God is all-powerful, "they knew it and they demonstratively proved it" (*In III Sent.*, d. 23, q. 3, a. 2, ad 3m). Cf. *op. cit.*, III, d. 24, q. 1, a. 3, ad 3, solutio, a list of demonstrable preambles to faith: "Deum esse, et Deum esse unum, incorporeum, intelligentem et alia hujusmodi." His criterion is simple; if one pagan philosopher has reached any one of those conclusions, it is proof that natural reason unaided by faith is able to know it.

[5] A typical instance will be given presently: the natural light of reason cannot discover that the felicity of man will consist in the vision of God face to face, but reason can demonstrate that, failing the beatific vision, ultimate felicity is inaccessible to man. Another instructive case is that of Book III, ch. 159, where Thomas undertakes to prove that "it is rational to impute to a man his non-conversion to God even though he could not do so without grace." This is a rational answer to a question which, left to itself, reason could not even ask.

[6] *Contra gentiles*, IV, 1, 11. In no one of its four books does the *Contra gentiles* leave reason without faith or faith without reason. The first three books deal with "that truth which faith professes and reason investigates." Thomas does this by advancing reasons, either demonstrative or probable, borrowed from the philosophers or from Christian authors (a rare case, under the pen of Thomas, of the classical distinction between the *philosophi* and the *sancti*). The fourth and last book, which argues from faith, uses reason to answer the objections directed against faith by its adversaries and to confirm it by probable arguments only (*Contra gentiles*, IV, 9, 3). The revealed matter that surpasses reason (the "revealed" property so called) is distributed by Thomas Aquinas under three main headings: (1) the truth about God himself that surpasses reason, such as the Trinity; (2) the works of God that surpass reason, such as the Incarnation and its consequences; (3) that which surpasses reason in the ultimate end of man, such as the resurrection of the bodies and their glorified condition, as well as the rewards and punishments in future life (*op. cit.*, IV, 1, 11).

[7] *Contra gentiles*, II, 45, 9.

[8] *Contra gentiles*, II, 46.

[9] *Contra gentiles*, II, 46, 1.

[10] *Contra gentiles*, II, 46, 6.

[11] *Contra gentiles*, III, 37, 4.

[12] *Contra gentiles*, III, 17, 9.

[13] *Contra gentiles*, III, 17, 10, quoting Apocalypse 22:13.

[14] *Contra gentiles*, III, 26, 1. The chapters of *Contra*

Gentiles, III, 16 to 25, are a paraphrase of one paragraph of Denis, *De divinis nominibus*, 24.

[15] *Contra gentiles*, III, 21, 8, quoting Denis, *On the Celestial Hierarchy*, III, 2; in Migne, *Patrologia Graeca*, III, col. 165.

[16] *Contra gentiles*, III, 24, 5; *op. cit.*, III, 25, 1.

[17] *Contra gentiles*, III, 25, 4.

[18] *Contra gentiles*, III, 25, 8.

[19] *Contra gentiles*, III, 25, 9.

[20] *Contra gentiles*, III, 25, 11.

[21] *Contra gentiles*, III, 25, 11: "Therefore man naturally desires, as his ultimate end, to know the first cause, but the first cause of all things is God."

[22] *Summa theologiae*, I, 1, 8, ad 2m. Literally: "Cum gratia non tollat naturam, sed perficiat . . ." Observe the immediate application Thomas makes of the principle: "Because grace does not destroy nature, but perfects it, natural reason must minister to faith as the natural inclination of the will ministers to charity." There is the parallelism in *op. cit.*, I, 2, 2, ad 1m: "faith presupposes natural knowledge, even as grace presupposes nature and perfection the perfectible." And this extraordinary formula is given in *In Boet. de Trinit.*, prooem., 2, 3, resp.: "Continent tamen (ea quae sunt philosophiae) quasdam similitudines eorum (quae sunt fidei) et quaedam ad ea praeambula sicut natura praeambula est ad gratiam."

[23] Even without the revelation of the Gospel, and apart from the beatific vision, that quest would not be in vain. The Greek philosophers, particularly Aristotle, found a certain felicity in their philosophical contemplation of God. This may even be the reason God has created a world so conceived that, a *creatura mundi*, natural reason could know his existence and some of his invisible properties: "Sed quia perfectum hominis bonum est, ut quoquo modo Deum cognoscat, *ne tam nobilis creatura omnino in vanum esse videretur, velut finem proprium attingere non valens,* datur homini quaedam via per quam in Dei cognitionem ascendere possit" (*Contra gentiles*, IV, 1, 1). Philosophy is the imperfect fulfillment of man's natural desire to see God.

[24] *Contra gentiles*, III, 48, 15: "In quo satis apparet quantam angustiam patiebantur hinc inde eorum praeclara ingenia." The next sentence has *"quantas angustias."* The translators hesitate between various renderings of the word *angustia*. Some say "anguish"; others, finding this word too strong, use "narrowness of viewpoint," which is decidedly weak. The narrowness is not at stake, but rather the trouble it causes; *in angustiis esse*, "to be in trouble."

[25] "Cum autem impossibile sit naturale desiderium esse inane [a philosophical notion borrowed from Aristotle], quod quidem esset si non esset possibile pervenire ad divinam substantiam intelligendam, quod naturaliter omnes mentes desiderant [a fact known from experience], necesse est dicere [a rational necessity] quod possibile sit [that is, compatible with the nature of the mind] substantiam Dei videri per intellectum, et a substantiis intellectualibus separatis et ab animabus nostris." *Contra gentiles*, III, 51, 1. Even then God is not known as he knows himself, but the knowledge granted to the mind wholly satisfies its desire to see the substance of God, so its blessedness is complete. See *op. cit.*, III, 51, 2; III, 52, 1 and 5.

[26] *Contra gentiles*, III, 54, 9.

[27] The whole doctrine is summed up by Thomas in one single sentence: "Ad septimum dicendum, quod quamvis intellectus noster sit factus ad hoc quod videat Deum, non tamen est naturale quod Deum videre possit, sed per lumen gloriae sibi infusum" (*Qu. disp. de veritate*, q. 10, a. 11, ad 7m). Our intellect was made for the vision of God, an end which is beyond the grasp of our nature and can be reached through the infused grace of glory only. That the First Truth transcends the capacity of the human intellect becomes an argument to prove that divine help is necessary for man to attain perfect happiness: *Contra gentiles*, III, 147, 3–5.

[28] "Omnis substantia est propter suam operationem" (*Contra gentiles*, I, 45, 6). This often overlooked principle commands the interpretation of the whole doctrine. In it, being only attains its fullness in its operation; for instance, the intellect is at its best in the act of cognition. In fact, actually to know is better than knowledge:

"Actus secundus perfectior est quam actus primus, sicut consideratio quam scientia" (*loc. cit.*, 3). Conversely, since to be is to be act, being is active by definition: "ex hoc ipso quod aliquid in actu est, activum est" (*op. cit.*, I, 43, 1). Cf. "actus autem actionis principium est" (*op. cit.*, II, 6, 7). The two aspects are seen in one single formula: "omne enim res propter suam operationem esse videtur; operatio enim est ultima perfectio rei" (*op. cit.*, III, 113, 2).

[29] The strictly historical description of the world of Aristotle given by Father Joseph Owens, without reference to Thomas Aquinas either in the text or in the mind of the author, shows why the theologian could perceive a deep kinship between his own Christian universe and that of the Philosopher: "Being is derived to all other Entity and to all other Beings according to the degree in which the actual permanence of the separate Entities is shared or imitated . . . The sensible thing, in striving after the permanence of separate Entity, imitates and expresses the permanence, the Being of the separate Entities themselves." Joseph Owens, *The Doctrine of Being in the Aristotelian Metaphysics* (2nd ed. revised; Toronto: Pontifical Institute of Mediaeval Studies, 1963), pp. 463–64.

[30] *In Boet. de Trinit.*, 6, 4, ad 18m: "Quamvis homo naturaliter inclinetur in finem ultimum, non tamen potest naturaliter illum consequi, propter eminentiam ipsius, sed per gratiam tantum."

[31] *Contra gentiles*, III, 56, 3. In the angels, the natural desire of God does not rest unless they see the divine substance. They naturally know God better than we do, but this is the very reason they desire to *see* him more intensely than we do.

[32] "Cum autem *omnes creaturae, etiam intellectu carentes*, ordinentur in Deum sicut in finem ultimum; ad hunc autem finem pertingunt *omnia* in quantum de similitudine ejus aliquid participant: intellectuales creaturae aliquo speciali ori modo ad ipsum pertingunt, scilicet per propriam operationem intelligendo ipsum. Unde oportet quod hoc sit finis intellectualis creaturae, scilicet intelligere Deum." *Contra gentiles*, III, 25, 1. Cf. III, 25, 12 and 19; and *Compendium theologiae*, ch.

104: "Est igitur finis ultimus intellectualis creaturae, Deum per essentiam videre."

[33] "Omnis intellectus *naturaliter desiderat divinae substantiae visionem.* Naturale autem desiderium non potest esse inane. Quilibet igitur intellectus creatus potest pervenire ad divinae substantiae visionem, non impediente inferioritate naturae." *Contra gentiles*, III, 57, 4; trans. Vernon J. Bourke, *loc. cit.*, p. 192.

[34] "Cum igitur finis hominis sit felicitas in quam tendit ipsius naturale desiderium, non potest poni felicitas hominis in eo ad quod homo pervenire non potest, alioquin sequeretur quod homo esset in vanum, et naturale ejus desiderium esset inane. Quod est impossibile." *Contra gentiles*, III, 44, 1.

[35] Natural possibilities not attended by corresponding natural powers, are technically called *obediential powers.* Only God can actualize such possibilities. Obediential powers can be actualized because of the all-powerfulness of God, who *de potentia absoluta* can always do with creatures what he pleases. In fact, because of God's wisdom (*potentia ordinata*), there is always in the obediential powers an aptitude to be divinely actualized. This is what Thomas intends to convey by saying that, for an intellect created in the image of God, the vision of God is a *possibility.*

Even the Incarnation (*miraculum miraculorum*) was answering an obediential power in human nature, and for the same reason it was fitting that human nature be assumed in Incarnation by the Second Person of the Trinity. In the case of the beatific vision, the fittingness is still more visible. The specific kinship between God and the intellectual substances created by him in his own image and in view of himself, permits us to say that "the divine substance is not beyond the capacity of a created intellect as if it were something altogether foreign to it." On the contrary, the divine substance is, in itself, the first intelligible and, with respect to us, the first principle of all intellectual knowledge (*Contra gentiles*, III, 54, 8). Obediential powers are of many sorts; in the present case, this power consists of a natural possibility intentionally created by God in view of its supernatural actualization by grace. The future beatitude of intellectual substances lies at the very core of God's great design in creating the world.

[36] *Nic. Ethics,* X, 7, 1177a 18; Matthew 5:8 and John 27:3.

Chapter III

[1] *Summa theologiae,* I, 44, 2. The same story is told in a more detailed way in the *Questiones disputatae de potentia,* q. 3, a. 5, resp. The references required for a historical commentary are found in Pegis, *Basic Writings,* I, pp. 428–29, notes.

[2] "Et per hoc dicit Dionysius, quod licet viventia sint nobiliora quam existentia, tamen *esse* est nobilius quam *vivere;* viventia enim non tantum habent vitam, sed cum vita simul habent et esse" (*Qu. disp. de potentia,* q. 7, a. 2, ad 9m). This is the famous passage in which, as it were incidentally, Thomas lays down the leading principle of his own metaphysics of being. The objection was already known to Denis, who reports it and answers it in his *De divinis nominibus,* I, 259–60; see the commentary by Thomas Aquinas, ed. C. Pera, O.P. (Romae: Marietti, 1950), 614–15. The best explanation of the doctrine I know of is found in the commentary to Denis's *De divinis nominibus,* V, lect. 1, ed. C. Pera, O.P., 635.

[3] *Summa theologiae,* I, 8, 1, ad 4m. More references, with a commentary, are to be found in *Being and Some Philosophers* (Toronto: Pontifical Institute of Mediaeval Studies, 1949), pp. 175–76.

[4] The complete formula runs as follows: "Unde, in compositis ex materia et forma, nec materia nec forma potest dici ipsum quod est, nec etiam ipsum esse; forma tamen potest dici quod est, secundum quod est essendi principium. Ipsa autem tota substantia est ipsum *quod est,* et ipsum esse est quo substantia denominatur ens" (*Contra gentiles,* II, 54, 5). Cf. "Non sic proprie dicitur quod esse sit, sed quod per esse aliquid sit" (*In de divinis nominibus,* VIII, lect. 1, 751).

[5] The paradoxical aspect of the expression must be excused. Its origin is a passage of the treatise of (pseudo-)Dionysius the Areopagite, *De divinis nominibus,* in which Denis himself qualifies his expression by

a "so to speak." See *op. cit.*, ed. C. Pera, O.P., in the text of Denis, n. 334, 3 (p. 281). After explaining that the distribution of his gifts by the all-powerful God reaches all things; that not a single being is left totally destitute of such gifts, since each one of them is given "the virtue of intellectuality, of rationality, of sensibility, of life or of substantiality," Denis adds: "and even being itself, if it is permitted to say so, holds its power of existing from the supersubstantial power." The Greek *dunamin eis to einai* is rendered into Latin by *virtutem ad hoc quod sit.* In his commentary, Thomas Aquinas accounts for the restriction introduced by Denis (*si fas est dicere*: "if it is permitted to use that expression") by the fact that, as mentioned above in note 4, properly speaking it cannot be said that *esse* is, but rather that by it something is: *ed. cit.*, 751, p. 283. Cf. "Virtus Essendi" in *Mediaeval Studies*, vol. 26 (1964).

⁶ *Contra gentiles*, I, 20, 24.

⁷ *Contra gentiles*, I, 20, 20.

⁸ *Contra gentiles*, I, 22, 5. Literally: "each thing is through its own act of being (*esse*)." Do not translate this statement as "through its own being"; the English word "being" correctly renders the Latin *ens;* there is no English word for *esse* used as a substantive, but being is that which has *esse.* So *esse* is not being, but rather the formal cause of being.

⁹ *Summa theologiae*, I, 3, 5, resp.

¹⁰ *Quaestiones disputatae de anima*, q. 6, a. 2, ad 9

¹¹ *In I Sent.*, d. 37, q. 1, a. 1, resp.

¹² Several months after writing these words, I received an unexpected confirmation of their truth. In a letter dated March 21, 1964, a theologian friend observed: "Doctrinal 'safety' is a still solid utopia. In an august and learned assembly, I have heard with my own ears this lapidary sentence: 'Haec quae dicit Excellentia X sunt quidem omnino vera, sed prorsus periculosa.' And the motion, too true but not safe enough, was pitilessly lost." If one were to say that in matters of doctrine nothing is safe but the truth, would that be an unsafe proposition?

¹³ *In I Sent*, d. 37, q. 2, a. 1, resp.

[14] "Ipsum divinum esse est sua essentia vel natura." *Contra gentiles,* I, 22, 10.

[15] "Divina autem substantia est ipsum esse." *Contra gentiles,* I, 23, 2. Cf. II, 15, 5.

[16] "Hoc autem, scilicet esse in actu, est ipsa divina essentia" (*Contra gentiles,* I, 24, 5). This does not mean, "to be in act" in opposition to "being in potency" but rather "to be in the full actuality of being."

[17] "Esse enim Dei est sua substantia" (*Contra gentiles,* II, 52, 9). For this very reason God is the source of actual existence: "fons essendi" (*op. cit.,* I, 84, 3); "fontale principium totius esse . . ." (*op. cit.,* I, 68, 3).

[18] *Contra gentiles,* II, 52, 9. My necessarily shortened and oversimplified exposition can convey no idea of the almost unbelievable ease with which Thomas is passing from one of the two domains to the other: "Therefore it is impossible that the substance of any thing other than the first agent should be being in itself. Wherefore in Exodus 3:14 . . ." etc. This "wherefore" or *"hinc est"* is truly amazing. Surely Thomas does not mean that the teaching of Scripture follows from the philosophical distinction of essence and existence that has just been established! How should it be understood? Probably in this way: Given that what precedes is what reason says, one is not surprised to read in Scripture that *"QUI EST"* is the name of God. The agreement of that twofold truth flowing from one single divine source was to Thomas admirable, no doubt, but to be expected.

The interpretation of Exodus 3:13–15 is the traditional one. Besides, it was the translation of the scriptural name of God accepted by Thomas Aquinas, whose doctrine is at stake here. Another interpretation has been suggested by some modern scholars; they say that in the passage in question, "far from consenting to express his essence in one single word," Yahweh refuses to do so. The text would then mean something like this: I am who am, and that is all you need to know. Cf. A.-M. Dubarle, O. P., "La signification du nom de Yahweh," *Revue des sciences philosophiques et théologiques,* 34 (1951), 3–21.

Without entering into discussion of the learned

120   *The Spirit of Thomism*

Dominican's arguments, I beg simply to quote the conclusion reached by a Hebrew scholar on the same problem: "With my investigation into the syntax of the passage I hope to have demonstrated that far from problematical, the 'existential' interpretation of the passage is the only natural and syntactically correct exegesis" (E. Schild, "On Exodus 3:14—'I Am That I Am,'" *Vetus Testamentum,* 3 (1953), 296–302. Suggested English renderings of the Hebrew name are: "I am (the) one who is" or "I am he who is." This, of course, does not mean that God has revealed to Moses any *metaphysical* truth; but it does mean that as a theologian Thomas Aquinas himself was well inspired in attributing to the scriptural text in question an existential meaning.

[19] *Contra gentiles,* II, 8, 4; cf. *op cit.,* I, 24. *Qu. disp. de potentia,* q. 3, a. 9, ad 22m. In this life the intellect operates as the form of its own body. The body does not share in the operation of the intellect, which in itself is a separated knowing power; but the intellect needs a material object as the starting point of its operations. The intellect, Thomas says, "non indiget aliquo corporali ad intelligendum . . . indiget autem corpore tamquam objecto," as sight needs something colored (such as a wall) in order to see color. Even after acquiring abstract cognitions, we need to imagine their objects when thinking of them again: "Et propter hoc exempla in scientiis sunt necessaria" (*loc. cit.*). This is the meaning of the well known Aristotelian saying, "One does not think without images."

[20] "Item proprium objectum intellectus est quod quid est" (*Contra gentiles,* I, 58, 5). The *quod quid est* is *what* the thing is, the essence or quiddity (the essence as expressed in its definition). "Quidditas rei est proprium objectum intellectus" (*Summa theologiae,* I, 17, 3, ad 1m). In this life the quiddity at stake is the "quidditas rei sensibilis."

[21] "Vulgi consideratio imaginationem transcendere non potest, ut ad rationem rei incorporalis pertingat." *Qu. disp. de veritate,* q. 10, a. 12.

[22] Such are the notions of angels, souls, intellects, concepts, meaning (including the meaning of meaning),

etc. In point of fact, considered in themselves, that is, apart from the individuals in which they reside, all essences are but imperfectly known. This is a much neglected aspect of the doctrine, yet it is there: "rerum essentiae sunt nobis ignotae" (*Qu. disp. de veritate,* q. 10, a. 1, resp.).

[23] Saint Augustine, *Confessions,* XIII, 31, 46: "per quem (spiritum) videmus, quia bonum est, quidquid aliquo modo est: ab illo enim est, qui non aliquo modo est, sed est est." This reading, as found in the M. Skutella edition (Leipzig: Teubner, 1934), p. 367, line 9, is the only correct one. The one that is frequently followed, "sed quod est, est," shows that the Augustinians can be as shy in following Augustine as the Thomists often are in following Thomas Aquinas.

[24] This is another instance of Thomas' arguing at once for the separate substances (angels) and for man: "Cognoscit tamen substantia separata per suam substantiam de Deo quia est; et quod est omnium causa; et eminentem omnibus, non solum quae sunt, sed etiam quae mente creata concipi possunt. Ad quam etiam cognitionem de Deo nos utcumque pertingere possumus; per effectus enim de Deo cognoscimus quia est, et quod causa aliorum est, aliis supereminens, et ab omnibus remotus. Et hoc est ultimum et perfectissimum nostrae cognitionis in hac vita, ut Dionysius dicit in libro *de mystica theologia,* "cum Deo quasi ignoto conjungimur; quod quidem contingit dum de eo quid non sit cognoscimus, quid vero sit penitus manet ignotum. Unde et ad hujus sublimissimae cognitionis ignorantiam demonstrandam, de Moyse dicitur, Exodus 22:21, quod *accessit ad caliginem in qua est Deus*" (*Contra Gentiles,* III, 49, 9).

The *penitus ignotum* is a Greek *pantelôs agnôston* which comes from Denis the Areopagite and, beyond Denis, from Proclus; see the commentary of Thomas on the *Liber de Causis,* prop. 6, ed. Saffrey, p. 43, line 18 to p. 44, line 16; the passage refers to the *Elementatio Theologica* of Proclus, prop. 123. Cf. "Primo enim modo (quando significat essentiam rei sive actum essendi) est idem esse Dei quod est substantia; et sicut ejus substantia est ignota, ita et esse" (*Qu. disp. de potentia,*

q. 7, a. 2, ad 1m); ". . . esse Dei est ignotum" (*ibid.*).

[25] *In de divinis nominibus, ed. cit.,* V, lect. 1, 618: "Hic Dionysius accedit ad exponendum nomen entis, secundum quod de Deo dicitur. Et quia, sicut jam dixit, non est suae intentionis ineffabilem Dei essentiam manifestare secundum quod in se est, sed secundum quod nomen entis, de Deo dictum, manifestat processionem essendi a Deo in creaturas . . ." Cf. *loc. cit.,* 610: "Nomen vero entis designat processum essendi a Deo in omnia entia et, secundum quod de Deo dicitur, est super omnia viventia." *Processum essendi* means *esse* as proceeding from God to creatures.

[26] "Solus Deus, qui est ipsum esse subsistens, secundum totam virtutem essendi esse habet" (*op. cit.,* V, 1, 629; *ed. cit.,* p. 234). On *virtus essendi,* see *Mediaeval Studies,* vol. 26 (1964).

[27] ". . . sed secundum rei veritatem causa prima est supra ens, inquantum est ipsum esse infinitum; ens autem dicitur id quod finite participat esse" (*Super Librum de Causis,* prop. 6; ed. H.-D. Saffrey, p. 47). Cf. *In Lib. de divinis nominibus,* ed. C. Pera, V, lect. 1, 635.

[28] See above, note 13.

[29] *Contra gentiles,* I, 25, 5. Cf. I, 26, 3, etc. *Summa theologiae,* I, 3, 3.

[30] *Contra gentiles,* III, 49, 9.

[31] *Contra gentiles,* IV, 1, 5–6.

[32] *Loc. cit.,* 11; translated by Ch. J. O'Neil (Image Books), p. 39.

Chapter IV

[1] "Ad secundum dicendum, quod quamvis non sit in potestate nostra cognoscere ea quae sunt fidei ex nobis ipsis, tamen, si nos fecerimus quod in nobis est, ut scilicet ductum naturalis rationis sequamur, Deus non deficiet nobis ab eo quod nobis necessarium est" (*Qu. disp. de veritate,* q. 14, a. 11, ad 2m).

The question is: "Is it necessary to believe explicitly?" The second objection runs as follows: "We have no obligation to that which is not in our power. But to believe something explicitly we have to hear it from

within or without, for 'faith cometh by hearing,' as is
said in Romans (10:17). However, hearing is within the
power of a person only if there is someone to speak.
Thus, to believe something explicitly is not necessary
for salvation." The answer is: "Although it is not within
our power to know matters of faith by ourselves alone,
still, if we do what we can, that is, follow the guidance
of natural reason, God will not withhold from us that
which we need." *Truth,* q. 14, a. 11, 2m; translated by
James V. McGlynn, S. J. (Chicago: Henry Regnery,
1953), v. II, pp. 258 and 262.

Incidentally, this should not be read as an expression
of theological liberalism, for of those who profess to
follow reason alone, very few are aware of the meaning of that simple formula. It means to live a truly
philosophical life, wholly dedicated to the pursuit of
truth loved for its own sake. Even among those who
call themselves philosophers, not all are able and willing
to do this. Cf. *Summa theologiae,* II-II, 2, 7, ad 3m.

[2] Charles Péguy, *L'esprit de système* (Paris: Galli-
mard, 1953), pp. 10–35, especially p. 12. Written *ca.*
1905, in a light vein, those pages well deserve to be
meditated upon by philosophers.

[3] Cf. "Franz Brentano's Interpretation of Mediaeval
Philosophy," *Mediaeval Studies,* I (1939), pp. 1–10.

[4] For references to this text and the preceding one,
see above, chap. II, note 28.

[5] "Manifestum est enim quod diversi actus diversorum
sunt; semper enim actus proportionatur ei cujus est actus.
Sicut autem ipsum esse est actualitas quaedam essentiae,
ita operari est actualitas operativae potentiae seu virtutis.
Secundum enim hoc utrumque eorum est in actu, essentia
quidem secundum esse, potentia vero secundum operari."
Qu. disp. de spiritualibus creaturis, a. 11, resp., ed. Leo
W. Keeler, S. J. (Romae: Universitas Gregoriana, 1946).

[6] *Contra gentiles,* III, 37, 8.

[7] *Summa theologiae,* I, 1, 5, resp.

[8] *Summa theologiae,* I, 102, 1, ad 3m. Farther on,
Thomas explains that since man, like the angels, was
ordained by God to beatitude, he should have been
created in the same place as the angels, which is the
heaven of the blessed, or the Empyrean. To which

Thomas answers that man was not created in the Empyrean, but will be transferred there in his state of final beatitude (*op. cit.*, I, 102, 2, ad 1m). This, of course, raises another question: where is the Empyrean? Even in the old cosmography, it was considered a "*caelum theologorum*," that is to say, a non-astronomical heaven of which science knew nothing and which was of interest only to theologians (Dante, *Convivio*, II, 4). However cautious he was in such matters, Thomas Aquinas imagined the Empyrean as an extra heaven located *above* the highest of the astronomical spheres. Now that those spheres have ceased to exist, nothing can be above them. It is up to the theologians to examine such questions.

[9] Emile Meyerson, *Identité et réalité* (Paris: Librairie Philosophique, J. Vrin, 1951), especially chap. I, "La loi et la cause." An extremely interesting contribution to a positive discussion of the problem—and openly concerned with the philosophical implications of science —is the article of another scientist: A. Metz, "Causalité scientifique et cause première," *Archives de philosophie*, 1961, pp. 517–41. Cf. E. Gilson, "Prolégomènes à la prima Via," *Archives d'histoire littéraire et doctrinale du moyen âge*, XXXVIII (1963), pp. 53–70.

[10] Jacques Maritain's contribution to the development of a moral philosophy is authentically Thomist in its inspiration and yet resolutely modern in its way of handling problems. It represents a deeply original part of his work. For an introduction to it, see Henry Bars, *La politique selon Jacques Maritain* (Paris: Les Editions Ouvrières, 1961), and also the same author, in his excellent *Maritain en notre temps* (Paris: B. Grasset, 1959), particularly chap. IV, "Passage de l'ésprit."

[11] Examples of those documents, which mark the opening of a new era in the history of Christian philosophy and theology, will be found in (among many other books) *The Church Speaks to the Modern World. The Social Teachings of Leo XIII*, ed. by Etienne Gilson (New York: Doubleday & Co., Image Books, 1954). A companion volume contains a similar choice for Pius XI: *The Church and the Reconstruction of the Modern World; the Social Encyclicals of Pope Pius XI*, ed. by

T. P. McLaughlin, C.S.B. (New York: Doubleday & Co., Image Books, 1957). The encyclicals of Pope John XXIII, *Pacem in Terris* and *Mater et Magistra,* attest the solidity of this recent tradition.

The Author

FOR MORE THAN half a century Etienne Gilson has been publishing the books and articles which have made him the foremost historian and explicator of Thomistic philosophy in our time. Author of several hundreds of articles and reviews since 1908, Dr. Gilson is internationally known for such books as *The Spirit of Mediaeval Philosophy* (1936); *The Unity of Philosophical Experience* (1937); *God and Philosophy* (1941); *Painting and Reality* (1957), and *Elements of Christian Philosophy* (1960).

Professor Gilson has taught at the University of Strasbourg, the University of Paris, and the College de France, and has been an exchange professor at Harvard University. In 1929 he founded the Pontifical Institute of Mediaeval Studies at the University of Toronto; he has been Professor and Director of Studies of the Institute since its founding. He was Gifford Lecturer at the University of Aberdeen in 1930 and 1931 and Mellon Lecturer at the National Gallery of Art, Washington, D. C., in 1955. He holds the Croix de Guerre and the Order of Merit (Bonn). A delegate from France to the San Francisco Conference, 1945, he was elected to the French Academy in 1947 and made a Senator of the Republic of France in the same year. In recent years he has resided part of the year in Paris and part in Toronto.